ALTERING THE EARTH

RICHARD BRADLEY

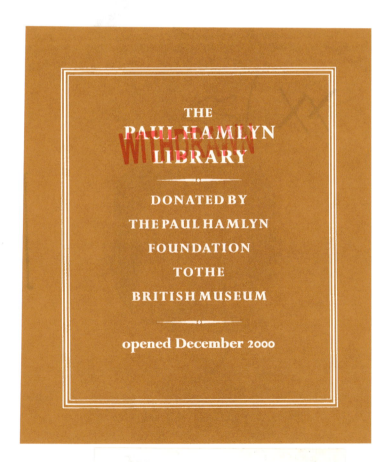

For Felipe and Ramon

RICHARD BRADLEY

ALTERING THE EARTH

THE ORIGINS OF MONUMENTS
IN BRITAIN AND CONTINENTAL EUROPE

The Rhind Lectures 1991–92

SOCIETY OF ANTIQUARIES OF SCOTLAND

MONOGRAPH SERIES NUMBER 8

EDINBURGH 1993

SOCIETY OF ANTIQUARIES OF SCOTLAND

MONOGRAPH SERIES

EDITOR ALEXANDRA SHEPHERD

British Library Cataloguing-in-Publication Data.

A catalogue record for this book is available from
the British Library.

ISBN 0 903903 08 3

Produced by Alan Sutton Publishing Limited, Stroud, Glos.

PREVIOUS VOLUMES

Number 1
CL CURLE
Pictish and Norse finds
from the Brough of Birsay
1934–74 (1982)
ISBN 9 903903 01 6

Number 2
JC MURAY (ED)
Excavations in the medieval
burgh of Aberdeen 1972–81
(1982)
ISBN 0 903903 02 4

Number 3
H FAIRHURST
Excavations at Crosskirk
Broch, Caithness (1984)
ISBN 0 903903 03 2

Number 4
JR HUNTER
Rescue excavations on the
Brough of Birsay 1974–82
(1986)
ISBN 0 903903 04 0

Number 5
P HOLDSWORTH (ED)
Excavations in the medieval
burgh of Perth 1979–1981
(1987)
ISBN 0 903903 05 9

Number 6
JA STONES (ED)
Three Scottish Carmelite
friaries: excavations at
Aberdeen, Linlithgow and
Perth 1980–86 (1989)
ISBN 0 903903 06 7

Number 7
C WICKHAM-JONES
Rhum: Mesolithic and
later sites at Kinloch.
Excavations 1984–86 (1990)
ISBN 0 903903 07 5

CONTENTS

Chapter motifs drawn from sites mentioned in the text – in order: Thebes, Kilmartin, Nether Largie, Poltalloch, Newgrange, Pierowall, Dundurn.

ILLUSTRATIONS

Cover illustrations: (front) 'Landscape of the Megaliths' by Paul Nash.
(back) Computer reconstruction of the Dorset Cursus.

FOREWORD

Professor Richard Bradley was invited by the Council of the Society of Antiquaries of Scotland to give the Rhind Lectures for the session 1991–2 and this volume is the result of those Lectures. In publishing them, we hope to bring them to a wider audience than the many who attended and enjoyed them in March 1992. We are grateful to Professor Bradley for all his work on the text and illustrations which has made this possible.

The Rhind Lectures are named after, and were endowed by, Alexander Henry Rhind, a prominent Fellow of the Society in the mid 19th century. He was born in Wick in 1833 and died tragically young in 1863, but in his 29 years he had achieved considerable success as an archaeologist, working both in his native Caithness, where, amongst other projects, he carried out a very competent excavation of the broch at Kettleburn, and further afield at Thebes in Egypt. He was deeply concerned with the wider issues of archaeology, including legislation on treasure trove and the recording of ancient monuments on Ordnance Survey maps, and his valued contribution to archaeology was recognised by his election as an Honorary Fellow at the early age of 24.

He bequeathed to the Society his library, funds for excavations in northern Scotland, the copyright of his book on Thebes and the residue of his estate of Sibster to endow a series of annual lectures, binding Council to appoint a Rhind Lecturer to deliver 'a course of not less than six lectures on some branch of archaeology, ethnology, ethnography, or allied topic, in some suitable place'.

The first Rhind lecturer, Sir Arthur Mitchell, was appointed for three years in 1876, and his Lectures were published in 1880 as *The Past in the Present*. Since then there have been Lectures on a variety of subjects by some eminent scholars, those in the last few years ranging from war and society in Early medieval North Britain to the archaeology of the Slavs to 19th century architecture in Scotland.

Richard Bradley has a thought-provoking and individual approach to the past, questioning received doctrine and offering new ideas. We are pleased to present Professor Bradley's Lectures as a volume in our Monograph Series – listening to them was a great pleasure, reading them will be a lasting satisfaction.

Anna Ritchie

President
Society of Antiquaries of Scotland

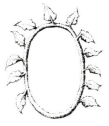

PREFACE

Alexander Henry Rhind was very much a student of monuments (Stuart 1864). He conducted fieldwork around his home in Caithness but also engaged in extensive research in Egypt. He was one of the first scholars to study the prehistoric temples of Malta, and he wrote about all three areas. Unlike some of his contemporaries, he did not feel compelled to trace these constructions to a common source. They were worth investigating in their own right.

He made the point himself in a letter to the Crystal Palace Company. They were planning to exhibit copies of ancient buildings from various parts of the world. Rhind urged them to include reproductions of the simpler monuments found in the British Isles:

> 'It is true that we may search in vain among the rude antiquities of our own land for structures which have any artistic beauty to recommend them, or which could produce the dazzling effect of the restored antiquities of the East; but then the gentlemen interested in the Sydenham Palace have wisely shown . . . that it is their design, not merely to gratify or educate the eye, but also to supply suggestive materials for intellectual information. It will not . . . be an objection to British aboriginal remains, that in an ornamental point of view they would be deficient, since, as practical and really attractive instructors, their value would be undoubted.'

When he died 130 years ago, Rhind bequeathed the copyright of his book *Thebes, its Tombs and their Tenants* to the Society. He also left a sum of money to finance further fieldwork on the monuments of north-east Scotland. That would be reason enough for talking about monumental architecture in the lectures that bear his name, but there was another factor that influenced my choice of subject. A few years ago I covered some of the same ground in a Munro Lecture given in Edinburgh, and I had long been planning to revise and extend that paper. When I received the Society's invitation, the opportunity could not have been more welcome. Without any hesitation I suggested that I return to the same topic. It was only later that I realised what a difficult task I had set myself. I could hardly have chosen a larger subject. Where should I begin?

From the start I was aware that I would be talking to a North British audience although most of my fieldwork had taken place in a marginal area far to the south. It was while I was thinking about my brief that I took a kind of working holiday, travelling along the west coast of Scotland with the Royal Commission's Inventory of Argyll. I went there to look at prehistoric rock carvings, but the lectures were

always in my mind. It was an opportunity to immerse myself in the archaeology of one part of Scotland, but as I walked around the monuments in this area, I was confronted by a question which would not go away.

Working in southern England, I am not used to the idea that the land is tilting. Scotland is coming up and Wessex is going down and that means that I was surprised by the wealth of Mesolithic sites surviving along the old shoreline, much of the way from Oban to the Solway Firth. I knew that occupation also extended inland, but such a concentration of material seemed poorly matched by the settlement record of the Neolithic period. And yet that was the time when great stone tombs were built. How was it that in one phase we find evidence of a stable coastal economy, but no sign of monuments at all, while in the next the settlement record is meagre but monuments are widespread (illus 1)? It was not a question that was peculiar to the British Isles, but it was one that seemed worth discussing.

1
Cairnholy Site 2, Dumfries and Galloway. One of the coastal distribution of megalithic tombs in southern Scotland. Photograph: RCAHMS.

As I visited some of these monuments, the questions multiplied, and with each fresh site I seemed to encounter more of them, until I realised that at last the lectures were taking shape. I have attempted to make those questions seem more immediate by explaining how each of them arose, in that way anchoring the ideas firmly in the Scottish landscape. Each lecture considers one aspect of prehistoric monuments and their interpretation and follows a train of thought suggested during the visit to Argyll. The lectures divide into two groups of three. The first group

considers the origins and workings of monuments, extending outwards from Scotland into Continental Europe before returning to a detailed study of some material from the British Isles. The last three lectures follow much the same plan but are concerned with the history of monuments, from the time of their original creation through to the post-Roman period. The final lecture was a little shorter than the rest as it was followed by a discussion, the point at which this English Bard, borrowing from Lord Byron, submitted himself to the Scotch Reviewers.

As far as possible, I have tried to retain the informal style of the lectures in the printed version and have added very little material. Each chapter begins with a summary of the lecture which follows and I have supplied enough references to allow the reader to pursue the issues in greater detail. These are not intended to be exhaustive: where I could do so, I selected sources with substantial bibliographies of their own. In making the transition into print I have been helped by many people, particularly the Editor, Alexandra Shepherd. I must thank John Barrett, Mark Edmonds and Mike Fulford for their comments on some or all of the original lectures and Sue Alcock, Lawrence Barfield and Sylvia Hallam for references that would never have come my way otherwise. None of these people is responsible for my mistakes. Most of the photographs were provided by Historic Scotland and the Royal Commission on the Ancient and Historical Monuments of Scotland, and I must thank David Breeze and Roger Mercer for making this possible. Those who were kind enough to supply the remaining plates are acknowledged in the captions. I must also thank Sonia Hawkes, Bob Wilkins and the Oxford University Institute of Archaeology for providing a fine copy of Paul Nash's 'Landscape of the Megaliths'. My greatest debt is to Margaret Mathews. Apart from illustrations 32, 35, 49 and 50, which are the work of Tess Durden, Margaret prepared all the drawings and coped with a wayward author who could rarely make up his mind. She produced clarity where there was chaos before.

Lastly, I must thank the Society of Antiquaries of Scotland for inviting me to give these lectures and for offering to issue them in permanent form. At times the prospect of giving six lectures in one weekend seemed rather an ordeal, but in the event it was a happy occasion. I am extremely grateful to the officers of the Society for their kindness and efficiency, and, most especially, for the warmness of their welcome. I shall always remember their hospitality during my visit. It reminded me how much I enjoy archaeology. I offer the text in the same spirit.

INTRODUCTION

MONUMENTS AND THE NATURAL WORLD

Monuments are not found universally and are rare among European hunter-gatherers. Using the example of megalithic tombs, the first lecture considers the origins of monuments and the ways in which they contributed to a new sense of time and place. There seems no reason to suppose that monument building was linked directly to the adoption of agriculture, and in certain areas the use of monumental structures may actually have helped to create the conditions for economic change. The argument is illustrated by megalithic tombs in Portugal, France and Scandinavia, and by the archaeology of Australia and the eastern United States.

◆ ◆ ◆

I shall approach my subject obliquely, through a novel and a painting. The novel provides the title for these lectures, and the painting supplies a metaphor for the archaeologist's understanding of monuments.

The novel is the last, unfinished work of the critic Raymond Williams (1989). He called it 'People of the Black Mountains'. Its opening volume is the history of one part of Wales told in a series of short stories, which start in the Ice Age and end with the Roman Conquest. In one of these stories, the inhabitants exchange red deer antlers with strangers who come from an area far away to the south east. Why do these people need so many antlers, they ask: 'Is it for the digging and shaping?' A visitor, who brings flints with him from the White Land, answers with the words 'We are altering the earth' (*ibid*, 149–50).

His reply gave me the title for these lectures, but I do not know whether Williams himself intended the words to have a double meaning. At one level, they seem to describe the process of monument building – the creation of mounds and ditches using antler picks – but they have a subtler resonance as well, for by building the earliest monuments people were indeed altering the earth, and in ways that meant that human experience would never be the same.

In writing the book, Williams was taking on a difficult task. He was trying to interpret the work of archaeologists, but he was also recreating prehistory in a particularly vivid way. We see this again in what he calls the White Land, the chalk of Neolithic Wessex, for this area provides some of the best known images of prehistoric monuments anywhere in Europe. Among them is an extraordinary depiction of the avenue at Avebury, painted by Paul Nash in the 1930s and later issued as a print (front cover illustration). In a sense this painting is more evocative than the

monument itself is now, and yet there is a different sense in which it is an act of the imagination, a recreation just as complicated as the scenes in Williams' novel. The picture has a strange history behind it, and this provides us with a metaphor for some of the things that we do when we study monuments. When Nash was working at Avebury the stones of the avenue had not been reerected. Some had fallen, others had been overthrown and buried, and they had to be found by painstaking excavation. His picture was based on the evidence of those excavations and not on the monument that we can see today (Stuart Piggott pers comm). Even before Keiller's repairs, the stones were raised from the ground through the power of the imagination. Yet there was nothing capricious about this, for the painting was based on sketches made during work in the field. This was a creative act, but of an archaeological kind.

The Avebury that we study today can only be reached by a rather similar process. It calls for an act of interpretation, and every generation makes its own. Behind that first attempt at re-creation, there extends an unbroken prospect of interpretation and reinterpretation. I want to suggest that this is a fundamental property of prehistoric monuments. It is at once an inescapable feature of their making, and a vital clue to their history. By building monuments prehistoric people **were** altering the earth. Not only were they creating an eye-catching spectacle that attracts the visitor to this day, they made their contribution to a new sense of time and place. And that was how these constructions played their part in the working of prehistoric society. Monuments are made to last, but their meanings are often elusive, and not just for archaeologists. The process of interpretation started as soon as they were built.

We have difficulty with this term 'monument', and our difficulties are worth some thought. The dictionary definition is rather neat: 'anything enduring that serves to commemorate'. Its root is even more revealing, for it comes from the Latin 'monere', to remind. Monuments are about memory: they join the past to the present. But that is not the way in which archaeologists have used the term. Monuments are also items of information. Thus we have Sites and Monuments Records, and, by extension, we have the prehistorian's idea of the monumental as something outrageous and massive which flouts the Principle of Least Effort (Trigger 1990).

So monuments evoke memory. Personal memories, no doubt, but to echo the title of Paul Connerton's book, how do societies remember (Connerton 1989; cf Melion and Küchler 1991)? One of the main ways in which they do so is through rituals. Among other things, ritual is a specialised kind of communication, and it is one that can embody a different sense of time from everyday affairs. In ritual the past reaches right into the present, and the two cannot be separated. It is a source of timeless propositions about the world, of eternal verities whose authority is guarded by specialised methods of communication. Rituals follow a set pattern and may communicate through unusual media such as song or dance. They can employ forms of language that are not in everyday use, and the texts can be performed using postures, gestures and movements which cannot easily be changed

(Bloch 1989). For Connerton, the physical element in such a performance is an important part of the way in which it is committed to memory.

An example may be helpful here (illus 2). Until the Reformation the Christian liturgy was conducted in a language that no one had used in ordinary conversation for centuries. Even now those taking part in the liturgy occupy prescribed places

2
Interior view of
Dunblane
Cathedral.
Photograph: Historic
Scotland.

within an elaborate architectural setting and they move about that building according to an unvarying set of rules. Certain gestures are laid down – genuflection, the sign of the cross – and the service involves specialised forms of utterance, including prayer and plainchant. These fixed elements are at the heart of many public rituals, and they work in two ways at the same time. They make it more difficult for the participants to discuss what is going on, and in this sense they tend to protect certain ideas from dissent (Bloch 1989). They also contribute to the processes by which fundamental beliefs are memorised, so that they are transmitted from one generation to the next.

The form of the Christian church is inextricably bound up in that ritual (cf Graves 1989). It has a stereotyped ground-plan that helps to determine the pattern of movement during the ceremony. Different parts of the structure carry specific connotations and may be embellished by specialised images that uphold the tenets of the liturgy. Different groups of people can be divided from one another by screens, whilst the entire structure has a single alignment which it shares with the graves of the Christian dead. There are whole panels of stained glass telling sacred stories, and specialised fittings such as fonts or confessionals that are peculiar to this kind of building. At one level the whole structure is a mnemonic device, and strengthens the role of the ritual in presenting an interpretation of the world and the place of particular people within it (cf Kemp, W 1991).

In this sense rituals and monuments both have a similar effect. They are among the ways in which societies remember. It seems hardly surprising, then, that they should normally be studied together. But there is a danger in this approach, for the link is not inevitable. Rituals may be performed in many other settings, and they need not leave any trace behind them. Alternatively, societies may choose to forget their past and can build elaborate conventions around that process. The creation of the first monuments in fact presents a problem, and it is that problem that I want to consider here.

◆ ◆ ◆

We must ask ourselves what archaeologists do when they study monuments. In fact they take them as given: as arbitrary cultural traits that assume a curious life of their own. Compared with Christian churches, such monuments appear oddly inert. They have their different uses, but they always seem to be passive reflections of something outside: religion, burial, exchange, food storage, warfare. They can be organised into classes as if they were portable artefacts, and at best they play a part in studies of specific cultural regimes. Thus we have monographs on different types of monument, but fight shy of asking why it is that all of them have a relatively short history. There were no major monuments in Britain or Continental Europe before the Neolithic period, but no one has ever suggested that ritual itself is a late development; it is convincingly documented as far back as the appearance of Homo Sapiens (Mellars 1989). And if we do ask why monument building commences in the Neolithic, our response is curiously oblique. In fact we talk about farming, as if monument building was only a side-effect of agriculture. We may have asked **why** monuments were built: we are told how their building was financed.

Again, it seems more important to ask what monuments do. The dictionary defin-ition is straightforward. Monuments commemorate and they endure. These are the features that really need discussion. Their links with a particular subsistence econ-omy are a secondary consideration.

In practice the building of monuments imposes itself on human consciousness in three different ways. First, it creates an entirely new sense of place. That is not to say that societies who lack monuments exist in an uncharted wilderness, for natural places can assume just as much significance (Wilson 1988); the difficulty is in recognising this process through field archaeology. What is really new is the decis-ion to ground the experience of place in deliberate, human constructions, and this involves a different relationship with the natural world. Instead of creating an intel-lectual structure around the features of the natural topography, monument build-ing is a way of establishing or enhancing the significance of particular locations. Once that has happened, those places enter the consciousness of the people who live and work around them until the landscape as a whole is changed. These new configurations enter their world through their everyday experiences and in turn those people provide a commentary on what they see (Barrett in press).

The second feature that characterises prehistoric monuments is that they last for a very long time. This is a statement of the obvious, but it is one that must be made. The calibration of radiocarbon dates only emphasises the point. The extraordinary longevity of monuments is just as apparent whether they are used over a contin-uous period or are rejected immediately. In either case they come to represent a highly visible past, and one which is manifestly of human origin. Their very sur-vival across the generations demands a conception of time that goes well beyond the concerns of the everyday (Shennan 1983). By their very construction they are difficult to eliminate from human memory, but when that does happen it offers one of the most promising routes to the study of social change.

On the other hand, memory is unstable. Even if social traditions can be transmitted over long periods, studies of oral literature show how rapidly details are changed, even when this is not intended to happen (Finnegan 1977). Rituals and beliefs can also be manipulated more consciously to serve the changing needs of people in the present; to revert to an earlier example, despite the remarkable stability of the Christian liturgy, the same basic ideas are behind the Desert Fathers, the Renaissance papacy and modern Liberation Theology. Again the visible memorials of older generations cannot be excluded from account, and these have to be incor-porated in any interpretation of the world. That is to say, a monument may change its meanings from one period to another without necessarily changing its form. It can be adapted, it can be left alone, but unless it is actually destroyed, it is almost impossible to eradicate from human experience.

Taking those points together, we can say that the building and operation of monu-ments bring with them a distinctive type of consciousness. This involves a subtle change in perceptions of place, and the creation and use of these structures necess-arily inculcate a new sense of time as well (Criado 1989a; 1989b). This is a process that can never be reversed. In both cases it forged a new relationship between

people, landscape and history. That is why I have called the first lecture 'Monuments and the natural world'.

◆ ◆ ◆

None of these observations is new, and all might seem easy to explain in purely practical terms. That sense of place could be explained by the requirements of an agricultural economy. By building long-lasting monuments in the working land-scape, people might have laid claim to scarce resources. They might even have lent legitimacy to those claims through the physical presence of the ancestors. The argument has been used in Old and New World archaeology and is a familiar explanation for the adoption and distribution of megaliths (Chapman 1981; illus 3).

Changing perceptions of time might also be linked with the adoption of agricult-ure, for the production of domesticated cereals and livestock involves careful plan-ning, and decisions made by one generation may well influence the fortunes of their successors. Land is cleared and maintained over long periods of time; there is a sense in which it represents a substantial investment. Even on a shorter time scale, farming involves careful calculations as to the amount of seed corn to store for future use, or the right number of animals required to maintain a breeding population. In simple terms, farming instills a sense of the past at the same time as it necessitates judicious planning for the future (Meillassoux 1981).

Proponents of this interpretation contrast the sense of time found among farmers with that of hunter-gatherers. Hunter-gatherers, they say, operate across a far shorter time scale. Food is consumed as soon as it is obtained and there is no need to make a lasting investment in any particular area of land (*ibid*). Territorial boundaries are weakly defined, where they exist at all, and little attention is paid to ancestry and descent.

And that is the fatal flaw in the whole scheme. It places all the emphasis on one end of a continuum among hunter-gatherer societies. The groups who conform to this scheme are essentially those who practice what James Woodburn (1982) calls 'immediate return systems'. These are mobile peoples who do not store food and lack elaborate systems of ranking and descent. Genealogy is unimportant, and there is little concept of personal property.

On the other hand, Woodburn contrasts these groups with hunter-gatherers who practice 'delayed return systems', and here the easy contrast breaks down com-pletely, for these include people who practice a far less mobile lifestyle and whose economy is much more specialised (*ibid*). Social institutions are important, and in this case there is some evidence for the storage of food. Unlike hunter-gatherers who practice immediate return systems, these groups have a stronger conception of territory and also possess a more elaborate social structure. In terms of what I said earlier, they have a more developed perception of place and time.

There is no doubt that the contrast is a real one, but there is considerable debate about the relationship between these ideal types (eg Woodburn 1988; Headland &

Reid 1989). The scheme is essentially an extrapolation from twentieth century ethnography, and it is on this point that opinion is divided. Until quite recently, immediate return systems were supposed to characterise most hunter-gatherers; so much so that those with delayed return systems were considered as a special case and were not studied systematically. At the same time, it has become quite clear

3
Interior view of the megalithic tomb at Nether Largie, Argyll. Photograph: Historic Scotland.

that some of the groups once thought to typify the hunter-gatherer way of life had a complicated history of their own. Among them were displaced agriculturalists, or groups whose relations with the outside world had been substantially altered during the colonial period. As a result, some authorities even suggest that immediate return systems are a modern phenomenon, brought about by the impoverishment of marginally located societies during recent years (Tilley 1989; cf Woodburn 1988).

This discussion is of great importance to any account of the origins of monuments, but is there any way of resolving the debate? Brian Hayden (1990) describes some of the hunter-gatherers with delayed return systems as 'accumulators'. By this he means that they are groups within which certain individuals tend to monopolise particular resources, often deploying them for social advantage by providing feasts. He makes the important point that accumulators have a specialised distribution in both archaeology and anthropology. They are found in those environments where people can live quite comfortably off a few almost infinitely renewable resources. They are able to do this because there is no danger of exceeding the limits of the food supply, and this is why the increasingly extravagant accumulation and dispersal of foodstuffs can take place. Similar social mechanisms cannot be sustained in every area, and in many regions ecological factors alone exclude any system of this kind. The distribution of modern hunter-gatherers is quite misleading, as they have often been forced to settle unproductive areas. Even so, there is enough archaeological evidence to show that over substantial parts of Europe Mesolithic people were living in regions which are never likely to have supported this kind of system.

The contrast between hunter-gatherers and farmers is equally confusing, but in a quite different way. We have seen that not all hunter-gatherers were alike. The same is true of those groups that we describe as Neolithic. There is another important distinction to be made, and this will appear again in some of the other lectures. Our conception of the Neolithic economy is severely biased by the evidence from a few well-researched areas where fieldwork gives us a picture of unusual clarity. These include the Balkans and the great loess corridors of Europe, where we find substantial domestic buildings, together with evidence of cereal growing. This is best exemplified by the Linearbandkeramik. All too often that model is extrapolated into other areas until it arouses quite unrealistic expectations, expectations that are immediately dashed by the results of fieldwork. An inevitable disappointment ensues, for beyond the limits of these areas, in Scandinavia, Britain and western France, the expected pattern fails to materialise (Whittle 1985, ch 6). Very few domestic structures are known, and the economic evidence, from pollen analysis as well as carbonised plants, is meagre in the extreme. With the exception of Scandinavia, we are no better served by finds of animal bones.

In fact there are perfectly good reasons for this contrast. The Atlantic coastline had strong links with the West Mediterranean, where the adoption of farming was slow, and in any case Scandinavia, western France and the British Isles were not included in the first expansion of agriculture (Zvelebil & Rowley-Conwy 1986). When elements of Neolithic material culture did make a showing, the

Linearbandkeramik pattern was virtually extinct. By this time there may be signs of a more extensive system of land use which is hard to trace in the same detail as its predecessor. For our purposes, the important point is that it leaves us not with one major contrast but two. There is the distinction between what Hayden calls accumulators and more mobile hunter-gatherers, and there is is also the distinction between the core areas of Neolithic farming, like the Rhineland, and more marginal regions of Europe where elements of Neolithic material culture made their appearance without much sign of large-scale economic change. The importance of those areas is very simple, for it is here that some of the first monuments were built.

At this point Neolithic specialists are trapped in a circular argument. They have no problems where traces of farming survive, but in the margin, where these are often very limited indeed, they substitute the evidence of monuments. Humphrey Case (1969) treats these monuments as an indication of what he calls a 'stable adjustment', contending that they could only have been built on the basis of an agricultural surplus. Proponents of this approach then try to strengthen their argument by explaining why farmers **need** megaliths.

We have to ask ourselves two questions. Is monument building necessarily linked to the adoption of an agricultural economy? And even if a connection can be found, how do we account for the paradoxical situation that mortuary monuments - particularly megalithic tombs - tend to be distributed in the agricultural margin and not where we find the most convincing evidence of farmers?

To address the first question, we need to leave Europe altogether. I want to discuss the relationship between monument building and food production in two other parts of the world, and in doing so I shall suggest some ways in which the argument can be widened. After that, I shall return to the European evidence and offer a rather different perspective on the origins of stone-built tombs.

My examples are from two very different peoples, both of them hunter-gatherers. Among the Australian Aborigines the evidence for economic intensification comes late and is not very widely distributed (Lourandos 1988). For the most part the pattern of settlement was a mobile one and yet it included monuments. I shall discuss the relationship between food production and the organisation of Aboriginal ceremonies. My other example is the eastern United States, where the monuments have sometimes been compared with those in Britain and France (Bender 1985). In this case, my reason for discussing this evidence is that American archaeologists also have problems in reconciling the evidence of monument building with their information about the subsistence economy. Those problems are nearer to resolution than our own, and we can learn from that experience.

In each example I am using archaeological and ethnographic evidence as a platform from which to question our stereotypes. I am not suggesting that the material from either area can be used as a direct analogy. The Australian evidence is still

4
Comparative
plans of the
stone alignments
at Kunturu,
Western
Australia (after
Gould & Gould
1968) and
Wilmersham
Common,
Exmoor (after
Grinsell 1977).

rather patchy and has not been investigated on a large scale, but it is highly revealing. It is commonly supposed that Aboriginal culture involved a very close integration with the natural world and that the features of the landscape itself were charged with supernatural power (Layton 1986; Wilson 1988; Morphy 1991). In fact it would not be too much to say that this was an area in which natural places seem to have played some of the roles that were taken by monuments in Europe.

Now, we realise that this portrayal is too simple. It is certainly true that the major Aboriginal ceremonies did not leave much trace behind, but monuments **were** constructed on a limited scale. These include the low earthwork enclosures known as bora rings, standing stones, arrangements of cairns, and stone alignments, occasionally of some complexity (Flood 1989, 251–5; illus 4). In addition, natural

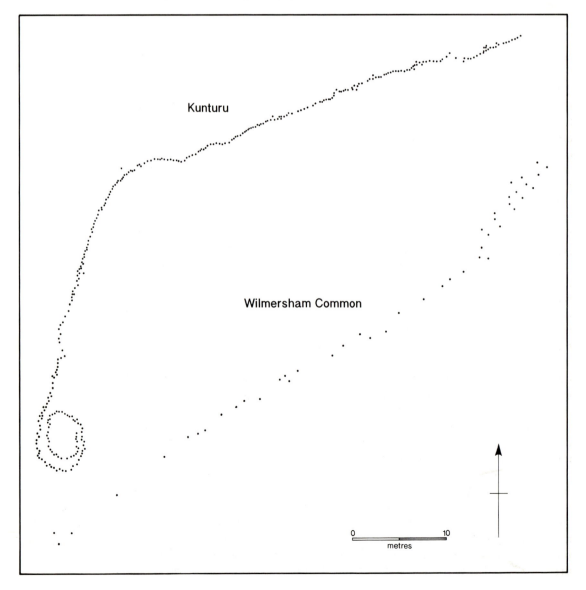

Kunturu

Wilmersham Common

0   10
metres

features of the landscape were embellished. Aboriginal rock painting is already well known, but another example is the practice of carving living trees.

The scale of these monuments is limited. The materials were readily available, and little effort was needed to build them. Their setting only emphasises the natural features of the landscape that play such an important role in Aboriginal belief. Those locations were modified to a very limited extent: this is particularly true of the carved trees. Instead of 'altering the earth', these structures still conform to its features. Even so, this example provides one important lesson. The building of small scale monuments need not necessarily be confined to sedentary peoples.

All too little is known of the circumstances in which these monuments were created, but again there is enough information to reject certain stereotypes. Although we might consider the Australian hinterland as one of the least hospitable areas imaginable, it was quite possible for substantial groups of people to assemble for ceremonies that extended over a considerable period of time. The slight monuments that now survive seem to have been built on such occasions, but their small scale gives no indication of the sheer number of participants. Two ceremonies recorded in Arnhem Land involved gatherings of two or three hundred people and lasted for more than ten weeks (Jones 1977). Things might have been very different. Had the participants devoted ten hours a day to monument building, their efforts would have totalled more than 25,000 worker hours. That is equivalent to the construction of three long barrows, a small causewayed enclosure or one of the lesser hillforts. The point is that they could have built large monuments, but they did not do so.

We must also ask how the participants were sustained over such long periods. Again the answer is revealing. They depended on what have been described as 'communion foods': large quantities of one resource amassed specifically to support a large gathering (Flood 1980). These included a number of resources that were harvested on a very large scale, and sometimes this process involved hard work and forward planning. Such foods included nuts, whose numbers could be manipulated by firing the vegetation; moths, which hibernated together in enormous numbers in certain caves; and eels, whose population was controlled by a system of artificial channels. In some cases these practices were part of a process of intensification that characterises the late prehistory of Australia (Lourandos 1988), but in these particular instances this investment of energy was simply to support the large numbers of people congregating for important ceremonies. In short, it would not be correct to assume that those ceremonies were the **outcome** of a buoyant economy; particularly in remote areas of the uplands, food production intensified to meet the needs of ritual life.

In the eastern United States the basic issues are simple. At first it seemed as if monuments originated at the same time as farming, but that argument has been largely discredited. First of all, there were cases in which the chronology of monument building raised problems because certain sites seemed too early to have been financed by large scale cultivation. This argument focused on the massive enclosure at Poverty Point and it resulted in the careful collection of food remains. The

results of this work upset many preconceptions. This was among the oldest cere-monial centres in the United States, and yet domesticated plants were never a major part of the contemporary economy (Ford & Webb 1956). Again it seemed likely that the earthworks of the Hopewell and Adena Cultures belonged to the first period of field agriculture in the eastern United States, and their appearance seemed to be linked with the general adoption of maize. This suggestion led to a massive increase in environmental archaeology, but its results are unequivocal. These great ceremonial centres were constructed **before** maize was in general use (Fritz 1990). In fact it was not cultivated on a significant scale until these sites were well established and some had been abandoned. What appeared to be the obvious relationship between resources and monument building was actually the wrong way round. With a growing commitment to field agriculture comes evid-ence of dietary stress (Perzigian *et al* 1984), and this may even have contributed to the demise of the ceremonial centres.

In fact it was only later, in the Mississippian period, that large monuments were erected by communities who were dependent on maize. The history of these monu-ments is a particularly revealing one, for the increasing dependence on a single resource, and on the fixed plots where it was grown, led to the spread of infectious disease (Rose *et al* 1984). There are signs of violence, and some of the ceremonial centres were provided with defences. One feature of those sites was the large scale storage of foodstuffs (Muller 1987).

It would be wrong to take this sequence, interesting as it is, as a direct analogy for what happened in Europe, but two comparisons may help us to put our house in order. In earlier periods we find that monuments were built on the basis mainly of wild resources; it is a moot point whether we call the population complex hunter-gatherers, or whether we think of them as incipient farmers because of the small

5
Comparative plans of the earthwork ceremonial centres at Seip, United States (after Greber 1979) and Knowlton, England (after RCHME 1975).

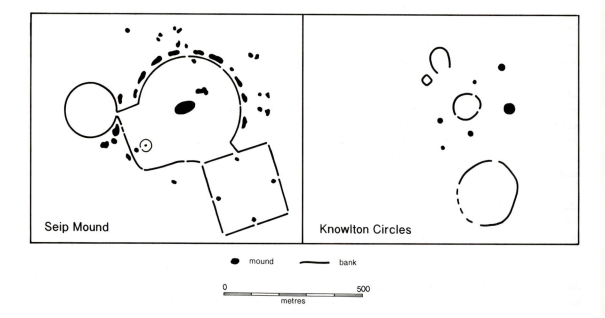

Seip Mound

Knowlton Circles

● mound   ▬ bank

0   500
metres

contribution made by domesticated plants. It may be better to refer to them as 'accumulators'. The monuments built in the Hopewell and Adena phases include mounds, enclosures and alignments of much the same size as those in Neolithic Europe (illus 5), and again they were among the nodes of an important exchange network. The later ceremonial centres were those built after the general adoption of maize. There might seem to be a link between the productivity of field agriculture and the construction of such enormous mounds, but in fact the relationship is problematical. The population was now more vulnerable to fluctuations in the food supply, and there are signs of warfare. The presence of massive foodstores inside these fortifications recalls the evidence of hillforts rather than henges.

So in neither case do we find what seemed to be the obvious relationship between monument building and the subsistence economy. In some parts of Australia, intensification was specifically intended to allow large ceremonies to take place, and these could happen in otherwise lightly populated areas far from the home territories of the participants. In the eastern United States, monument building preceded the general adoption of field agriculture, and when food production intensified it brought problems in its wake. So severe were these problems that they may have ended in disaster. If this really was the case, it might be wise to reconsider the links between farming and the emergence of monuments in Europe.

◆◆◆

That is an almost impossible task for a single lecture, but the one basic point can be made really quite simply. I am concerned with the **origins** of the earliest long mounds and megalithic tombs, and not with their successors. Once the principle of building mortuary mounds had been established, the same architectural ideas could be interpreted across the generations. It is quite enough to consider how that process began.

I am fortunate that Andrew Sherratt has been over much of the same ground in a recent article (Sherratt 1990). There he identifies most of the key issues. He has also made a number of points with which I would disagree.

Let us start with the areas of common ground. Sherratt's paper begins with two observations, both of which I share. The first megalithic tombs and their equivalents are a feature of the marginal areas of the European Neolithic: the North Sea and the Atlantic in particular. They are found beyond the limits of initial agricultural colonisation: that broad zone of settlement that focuses on the loess. At the same time, Sherratt follows the argument that the layout of some of these monuments made an explicit reference to the ground-plan of the long houses in that region (Hodder 1984). This is particularly important since these monuments lay outside their distribution. But we can also note that circular passage tombs, with no counterparts further to the east, are found along the Atlantic coastline.

Another feature links many of the places in which those developments took place. All are areas in which hunter-gatherers could sustain themselves without any pressure on local resources. In some cases their settlement sites have been investigated

in detail and provide evidence for a number of common features. There are signs that greater use was made of coastal resources (Zvelebil & Rowley-Conwy 1986). Some of the occupation sites seem to have been occupied for longer periods than their predecessors, and at different points along the coastline of western and northern Europe we also find the earliest cemeteries in those areas (illus 6). At sites like Hoedic, Teviec, Vedbaek and Skateholm there are patterns of association between particular burials and specific types of artefact, suggesting that we are dealing with the cemeteries of communities with well-established social conventions (Clark & Neely 1987). At a broader level still, we find evidence for increasingly sharp divisions between artefact styles in different regions, suggesting the emergence of groups who distinguished themselves from their neighbours through their self-conscious use of material culture (Gendel 1984; Larsson 1990a, 287–90).

It may be no accident that every one of these features is shared by the archaeological and ethnographic groups considered by Hayden in his description of 'accumul-

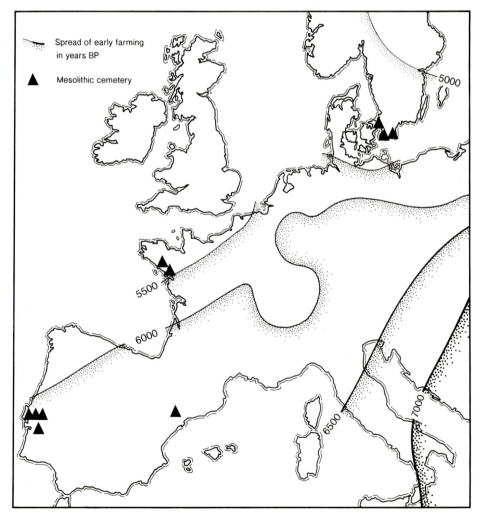

6
The distribution of Mesolithic cemeteries in northern and western Europe (after Zvelebil & Rowley-Conwy 1986) in relation to the spread of agriculture in radiocarbon years before present (after Ammerman & Cavalli-Sforza 1984).

ators'. They occupy environments that allow the accumulation of foodstuffs, together with their deployment in social transactions. Often they make use of marine resources, and again they are among the first groups to bury their dead with grave goods. One interesting feature which he also identifies is the domestication of the dog. This happens very widely in the ethnographic record, although the reasons for this practice vary. For our purposes this observation is striking as dogs are the only domesticated animals at late Mesolithic sites in Scandinavia and Portugal. At Skateholm they received formal burial in the same cemetery as their owners (Larsson 1990b).

Hayden suggests two other characteristics of accumulators. Members of these societies seek to raise their status by giving, by providing feasts and also by distributing exotic artefacts. In each case their aim is the same: to improve their standing by creating a network of debtors. Hayden argues that this practice may explain why they place such a premium on obtaining artefacts and foodstuffs that are not available locally. As he points out, there are many cases in which those foods are selected, not for their contribution to the subsistence economy, but because they are unusual or exotic.

Sherratt's paper shows that many of these conditions are satisfied by hunter-gatherer societies in the areas that saw the first megalithic monuments. Those in Western France seem to have been linked to the exchange network represented archaeologically by the distribution of Impressed Ware. In the same way, but at a later date, existing groups in southern Scandinavia were receiving axes from agricultural communities to the south. There is no doubt that domesticates were also adopted in these more marginal areas, although we know very little about the scale on which they were used. That is where the relationship between farming and megalithic tombs becomes so important, and it is where I part company from Sherratt's interpretation.

Let me quote his argument:

> 'The adoption of monumental tombs . . . seems to be characteristic of areas already fairly densely occupied by Mesolithic groups, who adopted Neolithic horticulture on the central European model. These tombs . . . were as basic a feature of early cereal cultivation as the hoe and the axe; the material infrastructure of the organisation of labour was as crucial in the establishment of horticulture as the more obvious elements of technology . . . The advantages of this form of organisation were not limited to the cultivation of cereals; and once established, could be applied to other modes of subsistence . . . where the recruitment of a more extensive labour force gave a competitive advantage' (1990, 149-50).

And again, perhaps more explicitly:

> 'In a society where labour was the most important commodity, moving large stones symbolised the workforce which could be assembled at any one time' (*ibid*, 150).

So the construction of megalithic monuments is a form of conspicuous display, but one which celebrates the cohesion of the agricultural workforce. Ultimately, as in so many explanations, megaliths play a useful role in farming. The sowing and harvesting of crops provide the motive force for everything else.

Is that necessarily the case? If we have followed Hayden's argument so far, why not go one stage further and see the creation of monuments as one more element in the playing-out of social relations? Long mounds may well reflect the characteristic ground-plan of long houses, and it is no longer so clear that they originated in the agricultural margin. They may have had a source further to the east, during the final phases of the Linearbandkeramik. Passage graves, on the other hand, should have a different origin. The chronological relationship between the two groups remains a matter for discussion (Kinnes 1992, 133–5), although Scarre (1992) suggests that beyond an area of overlap in north-west France, passage graves may have developed first, for in this case it is difficult to find any prototypes outside the local region.

◆ ◆ ◆

I must make it quite clear what I am and am not saying. I am suggesting that the creation of monuments could be another way in which local communities sought to gain prestige. The idea of building such structures could have developed locally, but it is just as likely to have been influenced from outside. The acquisition of more tangible assets from other areas might be part of the same process. But I am not arguing that this was independent of the adoption of domesticated resources; nor is there any reason to suppose that the agricultural margins were immune from colonisation. Neither proposition can be supported by the available evidence. My basic point is a far simpler one: the evidence for the **intensive exploitation** of new resources, or even for agricultural tasks requiring a significant workforce, simply has not been found – it has merely been postulated – and it is postulated as part of a legacy that we take for granted when we talk about the Neolithic period. Domesticated plants and animals are a feature of the 'Neolithic' economy; megalithic tombs, we say, are 'Neolithic' monuments. If we have one, we must have the other. In this case it amounts to saying that the presence of megalithic tombs is *prima facie* evidence of cultivation on a significant scale.

For people who could maintain a satisfactory lifestyle on the basis of wild resources, the large scale use of domesticates would have been problematical. I do not mean to suggest that agricultural techniques were difficult to apprehend or even to implement, but to do so on any scale would have involved a quite different understanding of the world, and of the relationship between nature and human culture. This is a theme that Ian Hodder has discussed in a recent book (1990). I have said that in Europe, monuments are not found before the early Neolithicperiod. That cannot be because people lacked the infrastructure needed to build them, since we have a growing body of evidence for relatively settled communities in the Mesolithic, some of them with complex social institutions. Perhaps the Australian example might be relevant again here, for in this case we considered groups of hunter-gatherers who congregated in great numbers to perform collective rituals, but left only the slightest monuments behind them. Like the sand paintings and earth sculptures created on those occasions, their impact on the terrain was very limited indeed. This may be because the major factor determining the location of these ceremonies was the sacred character of the landscape as a whole, and the particular potency of certain natural places. To engage in major modification of those places would have involved an entirely different attitude to nature. As Bird-David has argued recently, mobile hunter-gatherers may not distinguish between their own fortunes and the constitution of the world around them. They operate on the basis of trust: trust between one another on a day to day basis, and, just as important, trust between people and nature (Bird-David 1990; 1992).

I suggest that a similar reticence may explain the late date at which monuments were created in prehistoric Europe. The apparent synchronism with the adoption of agriculture need not be explained in functional terms at all: megaliths were not necessarily a way of making people good farmers. The common element is that in both cases the population was making a radical break with what they had known before. They were changing their attitudes to nature and the wild by domesticating plants and animals, and they were changing their whole conception of place by building megalithic tombs. **Both attest a similar change of attitude**, but the link was in the mind, not in the ploughsoil.

I quoted two case studies from outside Europe. Does the American experience shed any light on these problems? I believe that it may suggest a further possibility, for there monument building seems to have led up to the widespread cultivation of maize. I have already expressed my doubts about the directness of the links between monuments and agricultural production in Neolithic Europe. One reason for doing so was precisely because there is actually so little evidence for economic changes before those monuments were built; after all, some of them were constructed over settlements of entirely Mesolithic character. And unless that sequence can be shown unequivocally it seems implausible that they were made to celebrate the agricultural work force.

There is a wild teleology behind such ideas, and it should be resisted. It would only make sense if Neolithic people had formulated a strategy for economic renewal in which the best way to make agriculture work was to invent an ideology. It would be far simpler to see the creation of monuments as part of the logic by which accumulators pursue their social ends. In that case, is there any link at all between megaliths and farming? I suggest that one does exist.

In the agricultural margins, as I call them – those areas which were already occupied by stable hunter-gatherers – monuments and domesticates may appear at much the same time, but the first real signs of expansion, in the economy and in the pattern of settlement, come some time **after** the creation of monuments. If farming did not provide a surplus for building tombs could the sequence of events have been been the other way round?

◆ ◆ ◆

Earlier in this lecture I mentioned the idea that agriculture requires a different sense of time and place from hunting and gathering. That observation deserves our attention now. No doubt some hunter-gatherers opted not to move about the landscape, but at least they had the freedom of action to change their minds. That is not so easy for communities with a full commitment to agriculture. I also suggested – and this is the important point – that agriculture requires a quite different conception of time from the annual cycles on which so many hunter-gatherers operate. That change is not an option but a necessity, and again it requires a different kind of consciousness. That cannot have developed spontaneously. I argued that the sheer persistence of monuments would tend to inculcate a distinctive sense of place and time. This was not their intention, but it would have been one of their effects. Monuments, like so much of material culture, played an active role in the past. Could it be that the creation and operation of the first megalithic tombs was not in fact a consequence of economic change? In time it may have led to some of the changes of human perception that made agriculture both thinkable and possible.

Some years ago Colin Renfrew isolated five areas in which, he claimed, megalithic tombs might have developed independently (1973, ch 7). I am not persuaded by this argument, but it is certainly significant that in no fewer than three of these regions, Portugal, Brittany and southern Scandinavia, mortuary monuments develop in parts of Europe where Mesolithic cemeteries are found. In each case these are on the coast. The striking feature is that in all three areas the archaeological sequence is similar. The Mesolithic cemeteries provide evidence of social differentiation and are closely linked to settlement sites that could have been occupied over lengthy periods. In Scandinavia there is even some evidence for the circulation of

7
The entrance to the megalithic tomb of Anta Grande do Zambujeiro, Portugal. Photograph: Mike Fulford.

unfleshed human bones (Larsson 1990a, 285). This is also found at the late Mesolithic occupation sites on Oronsay (Mellars 1987, 297–9), and it is a feature that is more commonly recognised at mortuary monuments of Neolithic date. Yet in each of these areas the first evidence for agriculture on any scale is found in a later phase than the first of these monuments. In Portugal the oldest megalithic tombs belong to a period in which some sites provide evidence of domesticated resources whilst others are associated with wild plants and animals (Kalb 1989; illus 7). As Strauss (1991) recently pointed out, the most convincing signs of economic growth are found some centuries later, and only then can we show that domesticated plants made much contribution to the food supply.

In north-west France the situation is rather similar. A few of the first stone tombs may be associated with Mesolithic artefacts, even when there is pollen evidence for the presence of cereals (L'Helgouac'h 1976; illus 8). Our information is limited but whilst there are a few signs of land clearance at the beginning of the Neolithic period, the best evidence for a sustained human impact on the landscape comes at a later stage (Hibbs 1984, 275–6). Exactly the same sequence is found in the Breton uplands, and here the first pollen evidence for cereal farming appears some time after the construction of the earliest mortuary monuments (Briard 1989, pt 2).

In Scandinavia the evidence is of much better quality, but it shows exactly the same pattern. Cereals seem to have been available in small numbers during the late Mesolithic, and long barrows and possibly dolmens were built during the period in which material culture changed (Fischer 1982; Jennbert 1985; illus 9). But the major transformation of the landscape did not take place for several hundred years. When it did so, its effects were obvious. Large settlements appear for the first time and there are more indications of sedentary occupation (Madsen 1982). Cattle increased in importance over pigs, and, as Thrane (1989) has

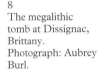

8
The megalithic tomb at Dissignac, Brittany.
Photograph: Aubrey Burl.

recently suggested, this is the first period in which we can recognise traces of plough agriculture. There may have been a similar sequence in Britain where our evidence is much more limited. Here again we find a major expansion in the number and size of settlement areas several centuries **after** the first construction of long mounds (Bradley 1987a).

Perhaps I have raised more questions than I can reasonably hope to answer, but some are more important than others and I need to summarise the points that I have made so far. The creation of monuments involved a subtle change in the relationship between people and the natural world. That change was just as fundamental as the adoption of domesticated resources, but whilst the two developments may have run in parallel, neither was simply a function of the other. Some monuments could have been built – and possibly were built – without the adoption of an agricultural economy. Some societies may have found it easier to make a significant commitment to farming because of a new sense of time and place imparted by the existence of monuments. Agricultural expansion did not precede the first construction of mounds or tombs as the model of 'stable adjustment' would suggest; if anything, the archaeological sequence is the other way round. Both farming and

9
Toftum long
barrow, Funen,
Denmark.

monument building involved new relationships between culture and nature, and together they amount to a process of 'altering the earth', but for that transformation to be thinkable at all required a quite different attitude of mind. That is really what constitutes the 'Neolithic'.

◆ ◆ ◆

Now these ideas are simply the preamble to a much broader case which I shall be arguing in the remaining lectures: that monuments must be studied in their own right and not as occasional indulgences made possible by growing prosperity. In the next two lectures I shall talk in much greater detail about the ways in which monuments came into being. I shall say more about the significance of natural places in the lives of mobile people, and the ways in which some of those places were transformed into monuments. I shall also say something about how the presence and operation of monuments affected human experience, and the intricate connections that we can trace between the manner in which these sites were used and broader patterns in the evolution of society.

That is my task in the next two lectures, and in them I hope to justify my claim that the presence of monuments contributed to a new sense of time and place in prehistoric Europe. In the second half of this series I shall show how that was adapted and modified. I shall describe the way in which one distinctive form of monument – the causewayed enclosure – was used in different cultural settings across much of Neolithic Europe: how it was treated as an idea. I shall describe the processes that took place during the development of monument complexes, and then I shall take the same ideas to their logical limits. I shall end by describing how monuments from a very remote past were brought back into commission in the early historical period as part of the process by which rising elites established their claims to political power. As so often, they did so by manipulating history.

I began with two works of art, a novel and a painting. Both offer an imaginative reconstruction of the past, and each in its own way provides a point of departure for this book. Raymond Williams described 'People of the Black Mountains' as a work of 'sourced imagination' (Evans 1987, 187). The term is very apt, and it suggests something of what I am attempting here. The strength of Williams' writing comes from the breadth of his interests: his lifelong involvement with questions of social theory; his reading in the archaeological literature; and his sensitivity to the qualities of particular places in the landscape. The last he shares with Paul Nash. I have described how Nash re-created the Avebury avenue in a painting before its investigators could reconstruct it on the ground, but his imagination was quickened by the precise observations that he made during Keiller's field work. His interpretation grew out of a respect for minute particulars. That seems a good programme for archaeological research, and I shall try to follow it in these lectures.

PLACES AND HUMAN CULTURE

Many monuments were constructed in places that had already acquired a special significance. This lecture considers the ways in which some of these locations gained an additional importance and shows how that process was related to the development of monuments. The argument is illustrated by the changing history of cave deposits, menhirs and rock art, all of which seem to epitomise a rather similar perception of the landscape. Some of those places developed into monuments themselves. Alternatively, relics of their original use could be transferred to new locations where they played a part in the creation of other monuments.

◆ ◆ ◆

For those of us who study the past it is disturbing when the remains of quite different periods look uncannily alike. For a moment we lose our bearings, and then our confidence returns. When we reflect on the experience, it is revealing to find the underlying reason for that resemblance.

This happened to me twice during my visit to Mid Argyll. The first time was in the churchyard at Kilmartin. In this case my attention was caught by a purely visual memory. It was here that I came across a remarkable collection of West Highland gravestones (Steer & Bannerman 1977; illus 10). For a moment I saw them as part of a tremendously long series of carvings. There on the slabs, surrounded by elaborate decoration, was a brief synopsis of the career and status of the dead person, portrayed in the simplest terms through depictions of a few distinctive artefacts. Sometimes there was also an inscription with a name. But behind those carvings seemed to lie a history of similar sculptures, not necessarily memorials, extending back in time from Pictish symbol stones to Late Bronze Age stelae, and, before them, to Neolithic statues-menhirs (illus 11). All these carvings share the common characteristic that they bear a symbolic message through the depiction of identifiable objects. That is not to say that these artefacts lacked a wider meaning. We cannot tell whether they stood for particular people, or even for supernatural beings, but the form that the messages take is very much the same. It embodies some of the properties of those characters and it fixes them at a particular place in the landscape. In the case of the Kilmartin grave slabs we can read the carvings in two ways: by deciphering the inscriptions on these stones, or by interpreting the messages expressed by the objects they portray. In prehistory one of those options is closed and we have only the artefacts to guide us.

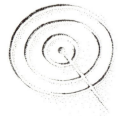

The second experience took place when I visited a prehistoric rock carving in the grounds of Poltalloch House (RCAHMS 1988, 123–4; illus 12). This lay on the edge of the garden, and like so many rock art sites in western Scotland, it was at a viewpoint. To the east it commanded a vista towards a henge monument, and to the

south it looked down a shallow valley to
the sea. There was nothing unusual in
this, except that the landscape around
the ruined mansion utilised the same
perspectives, so that the pattern of fields
and woodland on its estate was laid out
according to a rather similar axis. No
doubt this was coincidental, but again
the coincidence was revealing.

In this case the carving was wholly
abstract and had been applied to a natural surface. The rock cannot be identified from any distance, and forms an
integral part of the terrain. But whilst
we cannot supply a literal reading of the
design in the way we might read the
inscription on a gravestone, we can still
recognise a broader structure among
the petroglyphs. For example, in this
part of Argyll the carvings are larger
and more complex than those in the
surrounding area and include a significant number of elements shared with
passage tomb art (Bradley 1991). The
more complex carvings are certainly
found at viewpoints but they overlook
the main routes across this landscape
and, in particular, those leading towards
important monuments. In this case
none of the symbols can be identified
with a specific idea, but our reading
gains in confidence as we compare different carvings with one another.

In this instance the petroglyphs are
directly linked to particular places in
that landscape, but the carved stones
are fairly inconspicuous and can only be
interpreted at close quarters. Like the
archaeologist, a spectator would have to
move between the rock carvings in
order to understand their messages.
Both the grave slabs and the petroglyphs
are very different from the large constructions that I discussed in the previous
lecture. It is true that all monuments

10
One of the West
Highland grave-
slabs at Kilmartin,
Argyll. Photograph:
RCAHMS.

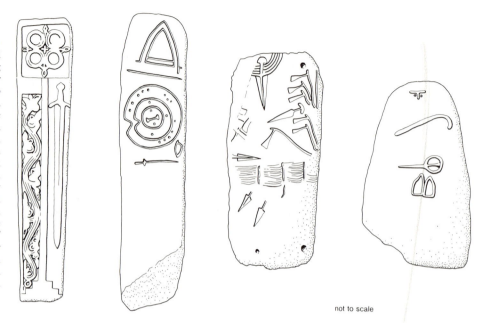

11
Monumental
sculptures depicting
weapons and other
artefacts. Left to
right: Kilmartin,
Argyll (Late
medieval); Santa
Ana de Trujillo,
south-west Spain
(Late Bronze Age);
Santa Verena,
northern Italy
(Chalcolithic) and
La Gayette,
southern France
(Late Neolithic /
Chalcolithic). (After
Steer & Bannerman
1977, Chenorkian
1988 and D'Anna
1977).

not to scale

occupy places within a larger landscape, but normally their construction changes the character of those locations. In these examples the effect is subtly different: particular places gain a certain emphasis, and they are inscribed with messages, but their meaning is transformed without any radical change to their topography.

◆ ◆ ◆

A similar contrast has been recognised by social anthropologists. We have already seen how formal monuments were a Neolithic creation and how their construction mirrors an altered perception of the world. Places, on the other hand, may have a longer history. They seem to be especially important in the lives of mobile people. To quote a recent study by Peter Wilson:

'The hunter-gatherer pins ideas and emotions onto the world as it exists . . . A construction is put upon the landscape rather than the landscape undergoing a reconstruction, as is the case among sedentary people, who impose houses, villages and gardens on the landscape, often in the place of natural landmarks. Where nomads read or even find cosmological features in an already existing landscape, villagers tend to represent and model cosmic ideas in the structures they build' (1988, 50).

Tim Ingold (1986) has made a similar observation. Paths are important to hunter-gatherers, but farmers place more emphasis on boundaries. This has implications for their perception of the landscape. Farmers control their land through its enclosure, but hunter-gatherer territories are very different – less obvious on the ground, overlapping and more informal. Hunter-gatherers recognise their territories by monitoring the paths running between specific places. Some of those places over-look the surrounding land, so that people may think of their territories in terms of the views seen from them.

Such ideas can be helpful, but they can also be applied too rigidly. Once again we are discussing ideal types as if the process of domestication brought an immediate change. That was not the case. In many areas agriculture was adopted only gradu-ally and there remained a contrast between the regions that were occupied year round and other parts of the landscape that were used only intermittently. The divisions between those two zones may have been extremely important.

In the first lecture I discussed some cases in which monuments appeared as early as any elements of Neolithic material culture, but there are many other instances in which natural places retained their significance for a long time. Sometimes these places were marked in archaeologically detectable ways – by carvings, by paintings or by the provision of special offerings – but there must have been many more which left no trace behind. In this lecture I shall consider some of the ways in which places acquired added properties, and some of the processes by which the associations of those places came to influence the construction and operation of monuments.

◆ ◆ ◆

For the moment we must go back to first principles. I have already suggested that public rituals may have been undertaken on some scale before any monuments

12
The prehistoric rock carving in the garden of Poltalloch House, Argyll. Photograph: RCAHMS.

were built, and that their creation involved a subtle change in the relationship between culture and nature. The existence of such rituals is by no means hypothetical. Quite apart from the evidence of Mesolithic cemeteries, there are a number of natural settings in which we find some of the characteristic features that identify later monuments: unusual deposits, specialised designs, restrictions of access and formal divisions of space. All of these are evident in the organisation of Upper Palaeolithic art (Leroi-Gourhan 1965), but the important point is that even if certain caves can be interpreted as some kind of sanctuary, they are not really monuments at all, for the entire system takes place within a framework provided by the natural features of the topography. That framework may have been selected, but it was not **created**. The physical features of these caves were hardly changed, and yet they allowed space to be used in a very structured manner, just like later enclosures or chambered tombs. For example, Barbara Bender has suggested that access to certain images may have been restricted as the paintings moved to more remote locations (1989, 87–92).

It is because so little attention has been paid to the ways in which hunter-gatherers treat elements of the natural world, singling some of them out for particular veneration, that the literature on prehistoric monuments can overlook those conceived on an informal scale, constructions that were little more than additions to striking features of the terrain. In this case the best comparison might be with the Aboriginal monuments that I described in my opening lecture. Any discussion that confines itself to the more conventional monument types – mounds, tombs, great earthwork enclosures – leaves out an entire class of archaeological evidence. Indeed, that class is hardly recognised for what it is because its elements are separated from the underlying pattern. The Neolithic and Bronze Age periods provide many instances of the special treatment of natural features. These are usually recognised, not because those features underwent any modification, but because they formed the focus for deposits of specialised kinds. Examples might include the placing of offerings in water, the accumulation of unusual artefacts at the foot of prominent rocks, or even their deposition in caves and fissures. The problem is that they are never seen as **parts of the same phenomenon**.

At this point some examples may be helpful. I shall begin with two cases in which we can follow the translation of a natural feature into the focal point of a monument. These are only instances of a much wider trend.

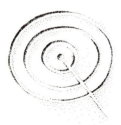

A particularly striking case is at Le Pinacle in the Channel Islands (illus 13). The site was originally interpreted as a settlement, but its position makes this very unlikely indeed. Like some of the places I have discussed already, it is in a remote location, and such a mundane reading of the evidence ignores its most striking feature: the extraordinary spike of rock from which it took its name. Recently Mark Patton has offered a new interpretation of the sequence, and I find this more convincing (Patton 1987, 91–2; Patton 1991). Its first use was as a stone axe quarry. Like the Neolithic quarries at Great Langdale (Bradley & Edmonds in press), its spectacular setting may have helped to establish the special importance of its products. After an interval the site was used again. Part of the promontory was cut off by a wall, and a stone platform was built against the rockface. This provided the focus for a series of unusual deposits, including a copper axe, a quantity of fine pottery, artefacts of Grand Pressigny flint and a large number of projectile points. Such deposits are not unlike those found in the henge monument at Newgrange (O'Kelly *et al* 1983; Sweetman 1985); the difference is simply one of history. The enclosure at Newgrange was constructed against the flank of a Neolithic passage tomb, but the platform at Le Pinacle was never more than an adjunct to the natural rock, and this was always the dominant feature of the site. It owed its importance to the character of the place itself, and possibly to its earlier reputation as a stone source.

13
Le Pinacle, Jersey.
The prehistoric
deposits were found
to the left of the
rockface.
Photograph:
Margaret Mathews.

My other example is Caerloggas on the edge of Bodmin Moor (Miles 1975, 24–50; illus 14). This site occupied a prominent hilltop with evidence of intermittent activity from the Mesolithic period onwards, much of it in the form of flint projectile points. Until recently it contained two enigmatic monuments. One was a low enclosure surrounding a natural tor. That rock had already formed the focus for a concentration of artefacts of various periods, but there is nothing to suggest that all of these were specialised deposits. On the other hand, the latest material on the site had a much more distinctive character and included a bronze dagger, a stone bead and a piece of amber, all of them items that would be more usual in a grave. The neighbouring monument was also associated with a long sequence of activity. In

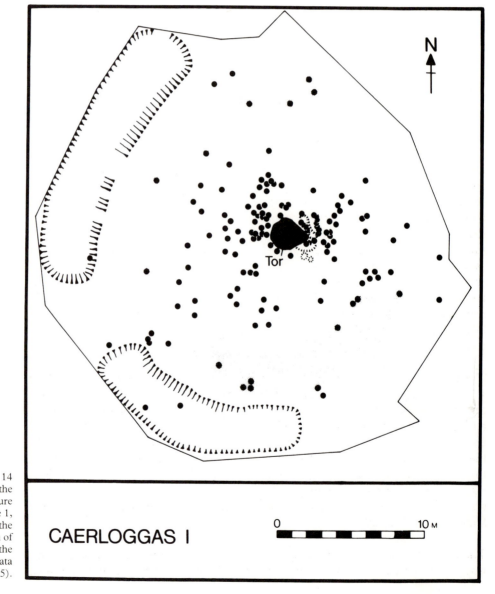

14
Plan of the earthwork enclosure at Caerloggas Site 1, showing the distribution of artefacts around the natural tor. (Data from Miles 1975).

CAERLOGGAS I

0   10 M

this case, the focus for the monument was a small upright stone, which seems to have been placed in position deliberately before the entire site was buried by a mound. In each example the existing features provided the point of origin for a conventional form of monument. In one case the natural rock, and the artefacts around it, were enclosed by an earthwork similar to a henge. On the other site, they were covered by a barrow.

Again I want to emphasise that the similarities between these phenomena far outweigh the differences. In both cases a natural feature of the topography seems to have acted as a focus for deposits of artefacts that might otherwise be found at formally constituted monuments. The sequence at Le Pinacle and Caerloggas suggests that that it was the long-standing significance of those places that led to their modification by earthworks and other features. To put it another way, this process effected their translation from the natural world to the world of human culture.

These examples illustrate my point, but they are only isolated instances. Having established what kinds of phenomena we should be studying, we must look at these issues on an altogether larger scale.

◆ ◆ ◆

Caves provide some of the best examples of the specialised use of natural places. A number of Neolithic sites in Italy have been studied recently and contain a remarkably consistent range of deposits (Whitehouse 1990; Skeates 1991). There are stone axes (O'Hare 1990, 136–8), fine pottery (Malone 1985, 135), animal bones and human remains. These may be located well away from the entrance, and the sites themselves can be inconspicuous and difficult to find. The pottery is of exceptional quality and is sometimes associated with striking natural features such as stalactites. The stone axes are often unused and may be made from attractive and uncommon raw materials. Human remains are found on many of these sites, and there is evidence of meat and plant foods. Their locations, however, would have been entirely unsuitable for settlement. Often they were hidden at inaccessible locations. They were hot and damp and, above all, they were cut off from any natural light.

The animal bones from these sites are of particular interest because they include such a striking mixture of domesticates and wild fauna. At Grotta di Porto Badisco the cave walls had been painted. The naturalistic paintings are all of wild animals and include hunting scenes, but in other zones of the cave they assume an abstract character. The depictions of wild animals are found close to the cave mouth whilst the others are in more remote locations, leading Ruth Whitehouse to suggest that the naturalistic paintings were accessible to people who were prevented from viewing the more specialised designs (1990, 26–7). As in many formal monuments, the distinctive layout of the cave would have helped to control access to particular knowledge and experience.

The chronological context of these sites is very revealing. They were used at a time when domesticated plants and animals had already been introduced, but their setting was generally in upland areas towards the geographical limits of the new regime. Such regions might have been used in the course of seasonal grazing, but they were at least as significant for their wild resources. In this way they were doubly marginal: cave rituals took place beyond the limits of the settled landscape and in areas where natural resources retained their traditional importance. As Whitehouse says, these sites were ideally located for encounters between two different worlds.

Their relationship with formal monuments remains a problem. They may have influenced the development of rock-cut tombs, but the most important character-istic of the cave deposits is that they were hidden from view. That is why so many of them have been discovered only recently. They occupy entirely natural places – places of a mysterious character – but their very location means that they are not apparent to the casual observer. In this respect they contrast completely with the evidence of megalithic tombs.

During the Copper Age, this division is complicated by the existence of statues-menhirs. At this time there were two burial rites in Northern Italy (Barfield 1986). One group consists of individual graves containing articulated corpses, together with a standardised set of artefacts: the male burials, for instance, are normally accompanied by daggers. Their distribution is interesting, as it hardly overlaps with that of multiple deposits, including those found in the caves (illus 15). Here

15
Chalcolithic burial traditions in northern Italy in relation to the distribution of statues-menhirs. (After Barfield 1986).

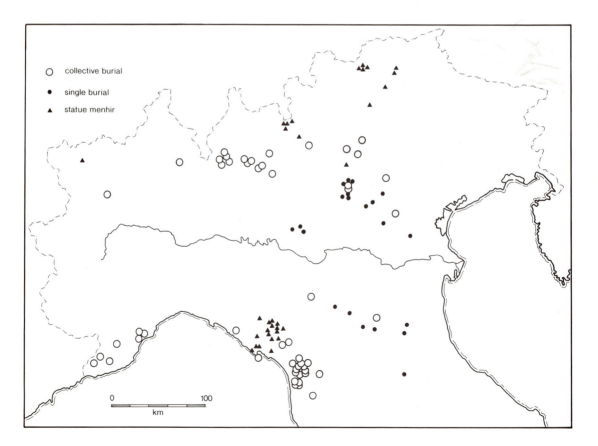

the organisation and contents of the deposits are very different. In this case more than one individual is represented, but just as important is the fact that the bones are mixed together and may well have been placed there after they had lost their flesh. Some of these deposits were unmarked, whilst others were in megalithic tombs. The grave goods differ from those found with single burials, and the most common items are beads. Daggers, on the other hand, are rare.

So far, that evidence might seem to indicate the existence of two cultural traditions, but certain features combine to suggest a more complicated interpretation. The distribution of the multiple burials closely matches that of statues-menhirs, which are virtually absent from the areas in which single graves are found. At the same time, these stone sculptures represent individuals with daggers of just the kind that are so conspicuously absent from the burial record. It is as if individual identities were mixed in the collective burials, where the deposits were concealed. Instead, the attributes of certain people – perhaps ancestors or mythical beings – were emphasised in a local style of sculpture. Lawrence Barfield makes the point that some of the same symbols are carried over into the rock art of the central Mediterranean, and that both groups of carvings may refer to the same ideology (*ibid*). The best evidence of such a link comes from Val Camonica where statues-menhirs of this kind are found near to the well-known rock engravings.

◆ ◆ ◆

A comparable system has been identified in southern France, and here there appears to be a rather similar link between the deposition of multiple burials in megaliths and natural locations, and the erection of statues-menhirs at significant points in the terrain (D'Anna 1977). Again, it seems as if individual identities were suppressed in the burial rite, whilst the attributes of particular people might have been associated far more publicly with specific places in the landscape. In this case there is evidence of occasional rock-cut tombs, although natural caves and the fillings of abandoned flint mines were also employed for burial (Colomer 1979). At Aven Meunier in Languedoc it even seems as if two of these decorated menhirs flanked the entrance to an underground burial deposit (*ibid*, 84–7).

The decorated menhirs of southern France divide into a series of well-defined regional groups, which are found in quite different kinds of location from one another (D'Anna 1987). For the most part they occur in areas with evidence of settlements and burials, but one of these groups is actually some way outside the distribution of contemporary activity, on the higher ground of the agricultural margin. In this case there are few other finds of this date, although they have been specifically sought. There is no clear link between southern French statues-menhirs and a local tradition of **rock carving** but recent work in Provence has documented the existence of a series of contemporary **cave paintings**. In this case the locations were easily accessible and not far away from the settlements, but there was no evidence that the caves themselves had ever been occupied (Hameau 1989). They contain small groups of artefacts and dis-articulated human bones. It may be no accident that the paintings incorporate some of the characteristic imagery of sculptures in the open air.

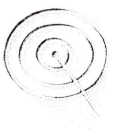

16
Sculpture of a
human figure with a
sword at Filitosa,
Corsica.

In all these cases the anthropomorphic sculptures have wider links. They mark particular places in the landscape and may endow them with a special significance. Some of those places were in areas with settlements and burial sites, but the distribution of these sculptures also extends to the limits of contemporary land use. At the same time, they ensured the presence of the dead in a setting where traces of the mortuary ritual could be hidden from view. In this sense they represent an intermediate stage between the specialised use of natural features of the terrain and the public architecture represented by megalithic tombs.

Elsewhere in the Central Mediterranean that link is made still more explicit. In Corsica there are a very large number of statues-menhirs, and these can be associated both with natural places and with megalithic structures (illus 16). In some cases statues of warriors even appear to defend natural strongpoints. The famous group at Filitosa seem to have been constructed around a conspicuous outcrop, but at other sites these sculptures can be found in rows leading up to particular tombs (Grosjean 1966; Camps 1988, 175–82). The chronological development of the statues-menhirs is poorly understood, with the result that we do not know whether such alignments might have developed over a long period of time. That remains to be established. What is clear already is that the Corsican examples span the full range of variation from places to monuments.

In each of these examples the sculptures in the landscape seem to refer to certain attributes of the dead, sometimes their role as warriors protecting the terrain. But that is not the only way in which they might be used. In contrast to the evidence from the Mediterranean, the decorated menhirs of Atlantic Europe may be linked more directly to the exploitation of the land itself. In this case chronological problems remain to be resolved, but some rather general patterns are already well defined.

◆ ◆ ◆

I mentioned the way in which particular places in the landscape could be used for offerings of Neolithic axes. This tendency is well illustrated in southern Brittany. The crucial period which saw the first adoption of domesticates also witnessed the erection of a series of menhirs (Giot *et al* 1979, 383–408; Patton 1990). Some of these were decorated with carvings of axes or even of domestic animals, and there are cases in which the stone itself had been shaped to resemble the form taken by an axehead (Bradley 1990, 84–5). At the same time, the landscape around these menhirs included a series of hoards, some of them containing axeheads set on end in the ground (Le Rouzic 1927). The choice of these elements for depiction can hardly be coincidental when those who carved these stones were making their first experiments with farming. Some of the menhirs may also have marked the long mounds discussed in my earlier lecture. As we shall see, these uprights came to play a formative role in the structure of megalithic tombs.

There may also be early menhirs in the British Isles, as one example on Anglesey was clearly slighted by the construction of a causewayed enclosure (Mark Edmonds & Julian Thomas pers comm). There is little way of dating these stones unless they

were decorated, and they may well have been erected over a very long period. But a limited number of menhirs, including some of those near Kilmartin, were embellished in exactly the same style as natural surfaces in the landscape (RCAHMS 1988, 126–43). In general these menhirs are located on more fertile land than the petroglyphs, and it seems possible that they were closer to settlement areas.

The distribution of Scottish menhirs can also be studied at a larger scale. Two important concentrations are found on the Rhins of Galloway and the Mull of Kintyre. Both are close to major groups of rock carvings, but their distributions complement one another. In each case this distinction seems to be related to the character of the surface geology. The rock carvings are discovered in areas with a limited mantle of glacial debris. The menhirs, on the other hand, occur where more of the surface rock was buried beneath a covering of till. In such areas it may have been simpler to mark significant places by extracting large pieces of stone and setting them on end: the standing stones in Galloway certainly include a number of glacial erratics.

—————————— ◆ ◆ ◆ ——————————

Such observations suggest that at one level menhirs and petroglyphs may have played rather similar roles in the prehistoric landscape; we saw other areas of overlap between these categories in the West Mediterranean. For this reason rock art is the other field that calls for extended discussion. It has a much longer history than the sculptures, but again the main groups of petroglyphs were created during the Late Neolithic, although the process clearly continued into the Bronze Age. Like some of the statues-menhirs, many of these carvings were at or beyond the limits of the land in year-round occupation. In the case of Scandinavian rock engravings they were often close to the sea. In all these areas we can say that they were on the edge of the domesticated landscape.

There are three main styles of carvings, and they are found in some of the regions which have already featured in this discussion: southern France, northern Italy and the Atlantic coastline. As we have seen, they are also found in Scandinavia. I shall have more to say about their subject matter, but they do share some common elements. Although there are areas in which the carvings are entirely abstract, they can also include the now familiar mixture of wild and domestic animals, as well as hunting scenes (Anati 1976a; Abélanet 1986; illus 17). There is no doubt that some of the petroglyphs also show farmers at work. This feature is found in widely separated areas, from the Central Mediterranean to Southern Scandinavia, but it seems less important when it is viewed in its local context. At Val Camonica, for example, Anati (1976b) considers that the petroglyphs exhibit a complex sequence in which hunting scenes were more important than depictions of agriculture until a very late stage, in the middle years of the Iron Age. The carvings at Mont Bégo are located well above the areas that could be used for growing crops (De Lumley *et al* 1976), whilst in Scandinavia rather similar scenes are sometimes found in regions where the soil was particularly difficult to cultivate. There are only eight depictions of ards in the whole of this region and there is no rock art at all in several of the areas that are best suited to agriculture (Malmer 1981, ch 6). These scenes no

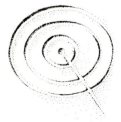

doubt encapsulated a view of the world that is lost to us today: in no sense were they simply illustrations of daily life. On the other hand, to those who created the carvings cultivation may have been a special event.

Unlike the decorated menhirs, petroglyphs are found very widely. Although they have a long history, they are normally located in areas a little outside the limits of stable agriculture. They may be discovered in regions in which the economy was largely mobile, or, more often, they occur towards the margins where year-round settlement gave way to patterns of seasonal land use, involving hunting or trans-humance. By contrast, they are rarely discovered in places with stable agricultural communities or patterns of fixed land boundaries. Their chronological distribution is interesting too, for the great majority belong to the Neolithic and Bronze Age periods, when they might be placed at or beyond the agricultural frontier. Almost without exception, they do not feature in the Iron Age, when there is evidence for a widespread intensification of farming (Barker, G 1985).

Again it is worth considering some examples in greater detail. A striking feature of the British uplands is the number of sites where Mesolithic flintwork has been dis-covered at the same locations as groups of later artefacts, in particular, arrowheads (Young 1989). These belong mainly to the Neolithic period and have a wide distribution. Their interpretation raises many problems, and so far there is no stratigraphic evidence to show that the ostensibly Mesolithic artefacts were in use at the same time as the other finds. It seems just as likely that they evidence the

17
Rock carving of human figure, horse and abstract motifs, near Campo Lameiro, Galicia.

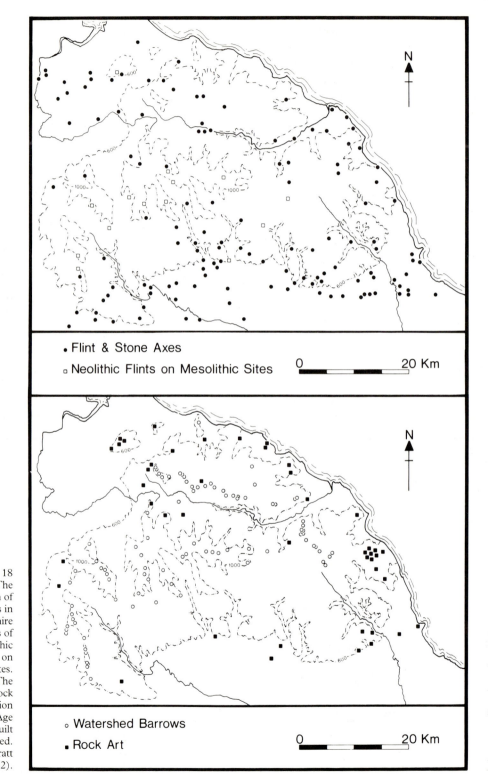

- Flint & Stone Axes
- Neolithic Flints on Mesolithic Sites

0 ——————————— 20 Km

- Watershed Barrows
- Rock Art

0 ——————————— 20 Km

18
(Upper) The distribution of Neolithic axes in north-east Yorkshire in relation to finds of other Neolithic artefacts on Mesolithic sites. (Lower) The distribution of rock carvings in relation to Bronze Age round barrows built along the watershed. (Data from Spratt 1982).

continued use of certain favoured locations for their wild resources. This could even have been combined with the summer grazing of domesticates. This zone of specialised sites is usually situated well beyond the limits of settlement and clearance, as it is reflected by discoveries of polished axes. In North Yorkshire, where this evidence has been assembled by Don Spratt (1982), there is a fairly sharp boundary between the two distributions (illus 18). Perhaps this was the meeting point between the domesticated landscape and the natural world beyond. It may be no accident that it is in this very area that a series of petroglyphs is found. Their precise date is a little uncertain, but the balance of probabilities favours an origin during the Late Neolithic.

Such carvings belong to a tradition that is widely distributed along the Atlantic seaboard, and some of the characteristic motifs are shared with other areas. Perhaps the best known of these petroglyphs are found in Galicia (Peña Santos & Vázquez Varela 1979), and here again we can recognise some evidence of spatial patterning at a regional level. One group of petroglyphs is located in the lowlands, close to the major fishing grounds, whilst the other is distributed around the fringes of the uplands in a setting not unlike that of rock carvings in the British Isles (illus 19). Rather more of the images found on coastal sites are in an abstract style that has features in common with the carvings in this country, but those found in the hinterland often combine the same motifs with depictions of animals. Again the distinction between the wild and the domestic seems to have been important, and many of these carvings can be identified as deer. The detailed location of the petroglyphs needs further study, but already they appear to share several of the features I have mentioned already in this lecture. A few of them are found at viewpoints or on prominent rocks, but in the inland areas where carvings of animals are

19
The distribution of rock art in Galicia. (Left) the distribution of abstract motifs and (Right) the distribution of animal carvings. (After Peña Santos & Vázquez Varela 1979).

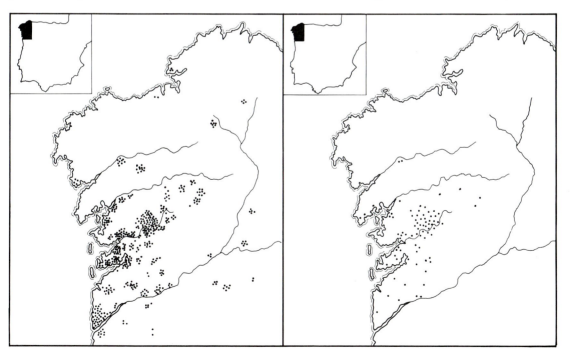

much more frequent, it seems as if these sites clustered around basins providing well-watered pasture or the paths leading through them to the higher ground. A similar observation has also been made in the Pyrenees, where the rock carvings are closely related to the main transhumance routes (Bahn 1984, 324-31).

At a still broader scale the distribution of rock art in Europe is very revealing indeed. Nearly all the carvings are found in what I have called the agricultural margins – the West Mediterranean, the Atlantic coastline and Scandinavia. Their histories vary considerably, but with the agricultural intensification of later prehistory these styles of rock art come to an end. We can recognise more local developments within this general sequence, for the petroglyphs in Scandinavia had a much longer history than those in Britain and Ireland, where the agricultural landscape was reorganised more extensively, and probably at an earlier date, than it was in Denmark and Sweden (Barker, G 1985).

In most regions the network of special places I have been describing was overwhelmed by the creation of conventional monuments. For example, in North Yorkshire, where those rock carvings had seemed to separate the lowland landscape from an area in which hunting maintained its importance, a whole series of round barrows were eventually constructed along the watersheds (Spratt 1982, fig 17; illus 18). Some of these may have been built in locations that were already important in human perception of the landscape, but at this scale such evidence is really rather elusive. We can shed much more light on the conversion of places into monuments by considering the later history of petroglyphs and menhirs.

When, a few years ago, we first found out that two of the great Breton tombs, Gavrinis and Table des Marchand, incorporated fragments of the same decorated stone (Le Roux 1984), the discovery was treated as altogether exceptional. Now we are able to recognise quite a few similar cases in which existing menhirs were taken down and their fragments incorporated into the structure of chambered tombs (L'Helgouac'h 1983). Examples of this practise have multiplied, and recent excavation has shown that sometimes these menhirs had formed freestanding structures at the same locations before those monuments were built (Patton 1990). At Table des Marchand it even seems possible that the tomb was built against one of those menhirs which was left in its original position.

There are also cases in which statues-menhirs are found within the structure of Neolithic passage graves. These may be free-standing sculptures, as they are in three of the chambers at Ile Gaignog (L'Helgouac'h 1965, 87), or they may be built into the junction between the passage and the chamber, as we find at Kercado (Giot 1971, 354). In each case the sequence must have been rather the same – the statue menhir was older than the tomb – but we cannot always be sure whether the megalithic monument was built around the figure, or whether the carving was brought from another location. At Déhus in the Channel Islands, the statue of an archer was certainly reused, as it formed one of the capstones (Kinnes & Hibbs 1989), whilst on a later site at Soto in south-west Spain a statue menhir was built

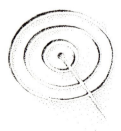

into the junction between the passage and the chamber (Shee Twohig 1981, 159–60). In this case it was turned upside down, and the original design was defaced and overlain with a new set of motifs (illus 20). This may seem like the opportunistic reuse of a convenient piece of stone, but quite often they are found in equivalent positions at different sites. They are located where the passage meets the chamber, but usually on the left hand side (Kinnes & Hibbs 1989, 163). Quite simply, these patterns of reuse must be more than a coincidence.

Similar practises seem to have been widespread and can certainly be recognised outside Atlantic Europe. Earlier in this lecture I mentioned the statues-menhirs of Southern France and said a little about their distribution. But I could have added that not all of them are in their original positions, for here there is similar evidence that existing menhirs were taken down and incorporated in formal monuments, sometimes as broken fragments. Such finds are poorly recorded, but in fact they occur quite widely. Twenty five of the anthropomorphic statues in Provence and Languedoc have archaeological associations (Jallot & D'Anna 1990, 378). Two are directly connected with open settlements, whilst another two are found in a similar context but had been reused. Four of the statues were originally associated with mortuary sites – multiple burials, an oval tomb and a series of cave deposits – and four more were incorporated into similar contexts after these sculptures had

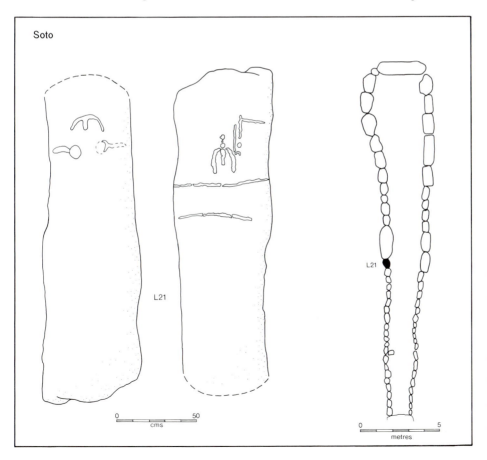

20
The reused carving in the passage tomb at Soto. (Left) A reconstruction of the carving as originally conceived. (Centre) The new carving created when the stone was inverted and incorporated into the megalithic structure. (Right) Plan of the monument showing the position of the reused stone. (Data from Shee Twohig 1981).

already seen an earlier period of use. They could also be incorporated into stone-built tombs and fortified settlements during a secondary phase; for instance, two of them were built into the well-known settlement at Le Lébous (Arnal 1973).

Rather similar developments are found in the southern foothills of the Alps and have been traced in considerable detail at Sion and Aosta. On deeply stratified sites like these the sequence emerges with a startling clarity. The lavishly decorated stelae at Sion were used and reused over six hundred years (Gallay 1990). The earliest examples belong to the same period as a megalithic tomb, but new statues were added during later phases which saw the deposition of a series of single and multiple burials. A significant proportion of these statues were subsequently damaged, and often their heads were removed before the fragments were incorporated in a further group of mortuary deposits. The sequence at Sion lasted for a very long time. The oldest feature is a megalithic monument which pre-dates the first of the statues by two hundred and fifty years. And after the final reuse of these sculptures the site continued in use as a barrow cemetery for another five hundred years.

The sequence at Aosta is almost as long, but in this case it has a different point of origin (Mezzena 1981). The earliest feature on the site was a series of stone-packed holes, perhaps for an alignment of menhirs. After a phase of ploughing – ritual ploughing according to the excavator – a small stone structure was built, associated with the first of the stone idols on the site and with deposits of human teeth. Later, a second series of stelae were erected. This time they were elaborately decorated, and it was only now that mortuary monuments of any size were created. In the following phase we find another series of stone sculptures, associated with depictions of weaponry. Further monuments were built, including a cist and two megalithic chambers, then the sequence was completed by the construction of a still larger cist reusing one of the statues. At Aosta these developments extended over six hundred years.

It is difficult to encapsulate such a complicated sequence of events, but the evidence from both these sites has some points in common. Again, the menhirs may have embodied the attributes of particular people and linked them with a specific point in the landscape. At Sion the first sculptures belong to the same period as a megalithic tomb, but at Aosta it was only later that the associations of those sculptures seem to have been incorporated in a formal monument. When that stage was reached, the carvings themselves could be defaced or broken. In that case the most important point is that for some time before any structures of this kind were built the place was already marked as somewhere special.

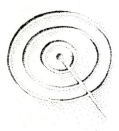

On sites like these we can read the changing relationship between sculptures and stone-built tombs in exceptional detail. They provide some indication of the real complexity of processes that in most cases are only glimpsed. But once we recognise the potential of this kind of evidence, other instances of this pattern come to mind. This is not a question of cultural affinities; these developments epitomise a similar set of principles. For some time it has been recognised that the decoration found inside the passage tombs of Loughcrew and the Boyne Valley has a lengthy history. Some of the stones at Newgrange and Knowth had been carved on more than one surface before they were employed in the monument (O'Sullivan 1986).

Those carvings that still remained visible after the tombs were built were replaced in a more ornate style. This has been treated as evidence for the evolution of megalithic art, but a wider issue may also be involved. Clearly, these pieces had not been detached from the living rock; they may have begun their career as standing stones. As we have seen in Brittany, once one example of this process is identified, others are much easier to find.

Rather later, in the Bronze Age, and in a very different area, we encounter my last example of this phenomenon. The extraordinary site at Filitosa in Corsica is perhaps the most convincing of this group of 'places as monuments' (Jehasse & Grosjean 1976, 102–4). It is set in the centre of a fertile valley near to the sea, and the local landscape is dominated by an extraordinary rock formation. This had already attracted settlement by an early stage of the Neolithic when a rock shelter was occupied. After an unknown period of time, but probably during a phase when Filitosa was no longer a domestic site, the same natural features attracted a different kind of attention. They became the focus for a veritable congregation of anthropomorphic sculptures. It is not known whether these accumulated over a long period of time, but the examples which have been assigned to the latest part of the sequence include figures with swords.

These decorated menhirs were not allowed to remain undisturbed for long. At a date which still remains controversial the rock was converted into a fortification, including at least two monumental towers. Small houses were built around their

21
View towards the crag at Filitosa showing the positions of the Bronze Age towers.

base, and the entire crag was enclosed by a defensive wall (illus 21). For our purposes the most remarkable feature of the site is the fate of the existing sculptures.
Some of these were taken down and used in the construction of the towers.
Although the excavator saw this as an act of desecration, I wonder if this is another
case in which powerful natural places were converted into cultural monuments as
relics of their former use were incorporated into the new construction.

◆ ◆ ◆

Petroglyphs were my other example of the way in which natural places might
become charged with an added significance. I think we can also see several ways in
which their importance influenced later generations. First of all, there is good evidence that the carvings that we think of as completed compositions in fact accumulated over a long period. There are striking contrasts in the degree of weathering
shown by adjacent motifs (Johnston 1989), and there are certainly a few rare
instances in which one image seems to be superimposed on another. This is found
in Scotland and Ireland, and also in Galicia. The origins of Atlantic rock art are
quite uncertain, although their closest well-dated parallels are found on the backs of
some of the stones incorporated into the passage tombs at Loughcrew, Newgrange
and Knowth. I have discussed this observation already, but even if it is treated simply as evidence of chronology its implications are profound. It suggests that some of
the motifs that characterise open air rock carvings were already current before the
full flowering of passage grave art in the Boyne Valley. If so, then one way of linking
these great monuments to earlier conceptions of the natural world may have been
by embellishing the tombs with a more ornate version of the carvings already current in the landscape. I shall return to this suggestion in my next lecture.

In northern Britain there are two kinds of evidence for the abiding significance of
rock art. Several of the round cairns in Northumberland seem to have been built
on top of existing carvings. Such evidence is little known and requires systematic
study, but already it is clear that some of the kerbstones had been selected for their
distinctive colour; for that reason it is most unlikely that these were simply clearance cairns (Stan Beckensall pers comm; illus 22). There is much stronger evidence that already carved fragments of rock were incorporated into Early Bronze
Age burials, both in England and Scotland (Bradley 1992). Some of the carvings
were old enough to be quite weathered, and many of the original patterns were
truncated when the pieces were selected for reuse. In a few cases it seems as if they
had been carved on opposite sides, suggesting that once again they may have
originated as freestanding structures such as menhirs. More often they appear to
have been stripped from the living rock; there may be direct evidence for this
process from the outcrop at Greenland (MacKie & Davis 1989). Although Colin
Burgess (1990) has argued that this happened by chance – these stones were
simply convenient pieces of raw material whose decoration had lost its significance
– the fact remains that these fragments are not a representative sample of the carvings found in the open air. There are too few cup-marks, and some of the more
unusual motifs shared with passage grave art are over-represented. Nor were the
stones used at random. Complex burials in cists were usually associated with cup-
and-ring-marks, and sometimes with rarer designs. Simple urned cremations, on

the other hand, might be covered by a slab bearing nothing more elaborate than cup-marks. There may have been a protocol determining how such pieces were to be incorporated into the fabric of these monuments. At its simplest this goes against the idea that older carvings were being reused haphazardly. Quite clearly, the different designs retained at least some of their original significance.

The same point can be illustrated by the placing of the carved stones in these monuments (Bradley 1992). Their kerbstones are sometimes decorated on the inner surface, and the slabs making up the cists were also decorated on the inside. In those rare cases where both faces had been carved, the more complex decoration was located in the interior. Each of these patterns would have had the same effect, for the decorated surface was directed towards the burial rather than the outer world. The same point can be illustrated at a still more detailed level. Loose slabs might be built into the body of the monument without any burials beneath them, but once again the decoration faced downwards. On two excavated sites in north-east England this even applied to a series of cup-marked boulders found in the material of the cairn.

Again I would draw a rather similar conclusion to my discussion of menhirs. Monument building involved a careful choice of location, but in certain cases relics drawn from other places might be incorporated into the project in a highly structured manner. It is difficult for us to reverse these processes, to establish the enduring importance of natural places when they are not embellished by the creation of monuments; but if we are to understand the complex process by which a wild landscape was eventually brought into the domestic world, the matter must be broached.

◆ ◆ ◆

22
A prehistoric cairn at Lordenshaw, Northumberland, apparently superimposed on a sheet of cup-marked rock. Part of the kerb around this cairn (not shown in this photograph) is also decorated.

That is what I have tried to do in this lecture, but I am only too aware that I have covered a large amount of ground, and so I would like to end by summarising the key points in my argument. All monuments were built in places, and many of those places were selected precisely because they already enjoyed a special significance. Our problem is in illustrating this point through archaeology. In some cases this is not too difficult. We have seen instances in which entirely natural features of the landscape had formed a focus for specialised activities some time before they were embellished by the creation of earthworks. But such a straightforward sequence is rather unusual. It is perhaps more common for natural features of the landscape to provide the point of origin of monuments. A good example are the cave deposits, and we saw how the collective burials found there can overlap with the contents of megalithic tombs and other sites. But at the same time we saw how the hidden world of the cave was supplemented by statues in the open air. In this case natural features of the landscape were not replaced by artificial monuments; they were complemented by them until they achieved a richer cultural resonance.

At another level, the siting of menhirs provides evidence for a distinctive perception of the landscape. They present the public face of rituals that were largely hidden from view and yet their siting in the open air helps to associate those practices with particular places in the outer world. In this case the attributes of the dead or supernatural beings were linked to specific points in the countryside. In the case of prehistoric rock art, that link to the natural terrain is even more direct, and in this case there is evidence that some of the petroglyphs were deliberately sited at viewpoints.

We can relate that observation to the distribution of these features. Rock art is found mainly in the agricultural margin where a mobile pattern of activity was especially resilient. The depictions of hunting scenes at some of these sites also suggests that they were associated with the limits of contemporary land use. At the same time, these special places would have been very important to those living in the core areas of settlement, and we have seen how widely fragments of already carved rock – both petroglyphs and menhirs – were incorporated into the fabric of formally constituted monuments. As often as not, they were removed from their original positions for that purpose. Nothing could show more clearly how significant they had become. It hardly matters whether we can read the messages inscribed on these stones. Their translation from natural places to monuments exemplifies a development of very much wider significance.

I have considered the use of a variety of special places in the landscape and the ways in which some of them played their part in the lives of different people. I have also argued that the existing power of those places had to be carried over into the building of monuments, but I have still to consider quite how those monuments were used. I shall do this in the next lecture.

3

MONUMENTS AS PLACES

Once they had been built, how did monuments work? This lecture considers the ways in which the creation and operation of large monuments affect human perception. Monuments are the outward embodiment of some of the most basic beliefs in society, and they tend to mould the experience of those who use them. They constrain the movements of the people who visit them, and provide a kind of stage setting for the performance of ritual and cere-monial. In this sense they can play an active role in the process of social change. I shall illus-trate the argument using the evidence of a variety of stone and earthwork alignments from the West Mediterranean to the British Isles. I shall also consider how the distinctions between monuments and the wider landscape were emphasised by decorative styles and by deposits of artefacts.

◆ ◆ ◆

So far I have argued that the first appearance of monuments in prehistoric Europe involved quite new relationships between people and the natural world. I showed the importance of natural places in a mobile pattern of settlement and described how at various times they became assimilated into the broader pattern of monu-ment building. Now I must take the argument further. I would like to consider two more questions: quite how the use of newly built monuments could influence human experience, and some of the ways in which people distinguished between the cultural space of those monuments and the world outside.

Mid Argyll provides an excellent point of departure. The area around Kilmartin contains a great array of monuments, as well as many important rock art sites. And yet on the ground we do not appreciate these monuments as so many separate constructions. There is an order to their distribution, and the whole is surely more than the sum of its separate parts. Standing stones, like those I discussed in the last lecture, are positioned in relation to topographical features, but they are also erected in relation to one another, so that they can form short alignments extending across the landscape. Sometimes those alignments are directed towards other features: prominent points in the terrain, or the movements of the sun and moon. The earthworks in this area also have their alignments, but of a different kind. The two entrances of the Ballymeanoch henge create a distinctive axis crossing the enclos-ure and running out into the wider landscape (RCAHMS 1988, 57). The Bronze Age cairns at Kilmartin establish yet another alignment running along the edge of the valley (*ibid* 14; illus 23).

We take such arrangements for granted. Their existence is uncontroversial, even unproblematical. But that is because as archaeologists we all too often reject our immediate experience of such landscapes and break them down into their con-stituent parts, so that the unit of analysis becomes the individual monument. When

we do so, we reduce our options dramatically. There are fewer questions to ask – when was it built? what was it for? – and any broader structures are lost. Such a timid approach to the archaeology of monuments reflects badly on the subject as a whole.

There is a site that exemplifies these problems precisely. This is the famous standing stone at Kintraw (RCAHMS 1988, 64-6; illus 24). Argument has raged about this complex (MacKie 1977, 81–92; Patrik 1981), just as it has extended to many of the stone alignments in the surrounding area (Ruggles 1984). Were they really directed at the movements of the sun and moon? Would the sightline have been obscured by prehistoric vegetation? Were Neolithic and Bronze Age people cap-

23
Air photograph
of the Bronze
Age linear
cemetery at
Kilmartin,
Argyll.
Photograph:
RCAHMS.

able of careful calculation? Were they undertaking scientific observations? These are legitimate questions but in some ways they are all too limited. If such interpretations are plausible – as sometimes they do seem to be – we overlook the fact that the operation of such complexes was first and foremost an experience. That is what visitors to Stonehenge on midsummer morning recognise and what its excavator seems to forget. Individual experience is at the heart of how monuments are used, and it is why monuments can be considered as a distinctive type of place.

In order to keep the argument within bounds, I shall confine myself to this one general category: the alignment or avenue. Again I shall introduce examples over a wide geographical area. Some are in Scotland, some in France, whilst others are in the Mediterranean, but when I talk about the relationship between monuments and the landscape outside them, I must focus on a much smaller area. The discussion will draw on the evidence of megaliths and enclosures, and in this case we shall consider material exclusively from the British Isles. The closing section of this lecture will build on what I have said already, by returning to the wider significance of rock art.

◆ ◆ ◆

What happens when a place becomes a monument? We have seen how it may be drawn into the world of human culture and change some of its links with the natural

24
The standing stone and other monuments at Kintraw, Argyll. Photograph: RCAHMS.

landscape. When we say that something is monumental, we imply that it is built on a very large scale. No doubt that is part of the answer, but in practice that change of scale is often combined with a certain formality in its layout; without that, typology would be an impossible exercise. Monuments impose order on the places in which they are built, and it is that new sense of order, as much as anything else, that we must consider now (cf Thomas, J 1991, ch 3).

Monuments orchestrate human experience. Their size is so important because it is one of the ways in which this is achieved; sheer size determines certain patterns of movement in and around a monument and rules out other options. As we shall see, this particular property of monuments, what WH Auden (1940) called 'the language of size', also means that particular information can only be obtained in a prescribed sequence. Monuments formalise a pattern of movement among those who are allowed inside them, and their features are as likely to conceal certain elements as they are to reveal them. A good example is provided by the Neolithic temples of Malta (Bonnanno *et al* 1990; illus 25). We might think of them as monuments that are designed to show off certain features, including their massive sculptures, but the basic configuration of successive courts and niches is equally well designed to restrict particular knowledge to those who are entitled to receive it. The buildings are not just a series of monumental backcloths; they are also a sequence of screens. To take the sequence at Hal Saflieni, in its earliest phase there were seven areas of enclosed space, but only two distinct thresholds to be crossed. It was a fairly shallow

25
The Neolithic
temple of Tarxien,
Malta (from
Zammit 1930).

structure. By the latest phase at this site the number of enclosed spaces had risen to fifty four and there were no fewer then eleven levels of access: eleven thresholds at which entry could now be denied (*ibid*). Monuments may offer a sequence of experiences to some people and exclude other people completely.

Because the participants are obliged to move around in order to view the entire construction, it is possible to manage their experience in several ways. Everything cannot be viewed at the same time, or from a single vantage point. A monument like Hal Saflieni may help to establish the sequence in which different experiences take place. It may also determine that different people have the same experience but from different perspectives: some closer and others further away. In this sense monumental architecture has much in common with the formality of ritual, and, like public rituals, it may have a critical role in inculcating the conventions on which social behaviour depends. But in the case of the largest monuments this process gains an added potency for those who have been involved in the very creation of these buildings. We know of many prehistoric monuments which made exorbitant demands on labour; the fact that they did so may have added considerably to their power to influence human conduct. As Ian Hodder suggests, the process of construction itself helped to create a sense of group identity (1989, 264–5).

The movement of the participants plays an increasing part in more extensive monuments, but it is also significant because one of the ways in which rituals are committed to memory is through the movement of the body (Connerton 1989). This is just as important to the creation of tradition as the correct forms of words. One reason for emphasising the importance of avenues and alignments is that their very scale, the distances over which they were built, makes the movement of the participants almost inevitable: they can only pass **along** such an alignment. The pattern is at its simplest here, and that makes our own task in recreating the working of these sites a little easier.

26
The fallen stones of the Pagliaiu alignment before restoration (after Grosjean 1972). Several of the stones (shown stippled) were shaped to resemble human forms and some (shown in black) were carved a second time to represent armed warriors.

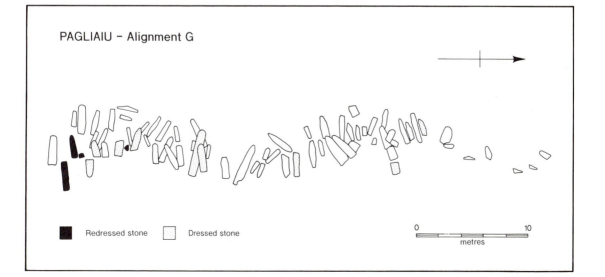

PAGLIAIU – Alignment G

■ Redressed stone   ☐ Dressed stone

0   10
metres

Towards the end of the last lecture I talked about the remarkable anthropomorphic menhirs of Corsica. These are very poorly dated and we do not know when their construction began, but some of the stone alignments on the island provide a simple example of how such monuments might work (Grosjean 1967). Alignments are very common and a number of them lead up to megalithic tombs, perhaps of some antiquity. Not all the menhirs in stone alignments are carved. As the observer passes along the main alignment at Pagliaiu (Grosjean 1972), not only do the stones get taller, they take on decorative attributes until they can be identified as human figures (illus 26). Three of the statues on this site can be recognised as warriors with their weapons. The anthropomorphic statues in Corsica may be taller than most, and those provided with weapons are the tallest of all. By moving along that axis the participant is increasingly overshadowed. The presence of stone built tombs at the some of these locations means that they are also made aware of the presence of the dead. Yet at the same time these figures form a kind of barrier blocking movement across the landscape. They follow a north–south axis, and the figures can face the same way, as if to confront the onlooker. That is a more complex arrangement than we saw around the crag at Filitosa. In this case, the alignment not only establishes a place as significant; it extends the significance of that place into three dimensions. In doing so, it lays down in greater detail how it is meant to be experienced.

◆ ◆ ◆

We can see this even more clearly if we think about other prehistoric alignments. Quite a number draw on natural features of the landscape, so that cursuses may run up to rivers, and stone rows can be aligned on hilltops. This is not an original observation, but in this context it is still important because it illustrates yet another way in which natural places might be drawn into a different kind of world. This is emphasised when we recognise that deliberately built monuments could be used in identical fashion, as if they were accorded much the same significance as those natural elements of the landscape. Thus, instead of running up to viewpoints, stone rows might be aligned on cairns or menhirs; instead of running towards rivers, cursuses can be aligned on enclosures or mounds. For example, at Carnac the great stone alignments incorporate the positions of at least two pre-existing long mounds of the type discussed in my first lecture (Giot *et al* 1979, 415–25). One of these was accompanied by a decorated menhir associated with a hoard of axe blades; this stone was also incorporated into the new alignment. In much the same way, the Dorset Cursus forms a link between a series of freestanding long barrows (Barrett *et al* 1991, 36–53). The same arrangement is widespread. We have already seen how some of the Corsican stone alignments run up to megalithic tombs.

To some extent such alignments create a link between different classes of monument, and between them and unaltered features of the natural landscape. But not all these effects could be viewed at the same time. In order to read these signs it would be necessary to pass along the body of the monument. These different links are created by the movement of the participants, and in the case of an avenue or alignment this could only be in one of two directions: any other options are excluded by the very nature of the monument. The result is a kind of stage-managing of experience.

I shall take the Dorset Cursus as an example (Barrett *et al* 1991, 365–8). This is defined by two parallel banks and ditches, nearly 100 metres apart, running straight across country for 10 km. In moving along the interior of this monument the participant passed through a series of experiences, and did so in a prescribed order. Let us suppose that he or she was moving from north to south, and to keep the argument within bounds, let us also restrict our account to the earliest phase of this monument. To begin with, the northern end of the cursus was difficult to find because it lay some way down the flank of a conspicuous ridge. When it had been located, it would soon become clear that this was done for a reason, for by offsetting the terminal from the crest of the hill, a long barrow three kilometres to the south appeared as a skyline feature. The cursus was aimed directly at that mound, which was incorporated in its path (illus 27). The alignment is very striking and its entire course as far as the barrow could only be seen from the terminal, an important point as the earthwork appears to have been built across a partly wooded landscape. But as the participants moved along the cursus their immediate objective, the long barrow, was lost to view, for it was concealed by the flank of the hill on which it was built. When it reappeared, it did so as a considerable mound blocking the path along the centre of the cursus. It also screened the other half of the monument. This could be seen for the first time from **behind** the long barrow, running across a broad valley and terminating on a second prominent ridge. Again that ridge was occupied by barrows of the same type. The terminal of the cursus itself took an unusual form, as if to echo the profile and alignment of those mounds. This would be rather easier to achieve as we know that this part of the complex was built in an area of grassland. In order to reach that terminal, and in doing so to

27
Computer reconstruction of one section of the Dorset Cursus looking south from its original northern terminal. The monument is directed towards a long barrow on the far skyline. Photograph: Thames Television.

pass from one pair of long barrows to another, it was necessary to ford a river. In this way the builders of the Cursus contrived a series of experiences for those who used the monument and determined the sequence in which they were encountered.

Much the same logic is behind alignments built on very different scales. At Carnac people would have been able to move along the stone rows, observing how these took their basic axis from much older monuments to the dead. As they approached the western end of the alignment at Le Ménec, moving uphill as they did so, they could see how it was directed towards an enormous stone-walled enclosure and how the stones defining the avenue itself became more massive (Thom & Thom 1978, ch 6). The approach to this enclosure was designed to overawe. Even on a far smaller scale similar effects could be created by the stone rows of highland Britain. Some of these also ran uphill so that the terminal, or the vista beyond it, was concealed from view. Others ran across the positions of cairns or cists, and in certain cases obstacles seem to have been placed in the centre of these rows, as if to make movement still more problematical (Emmett 1979).

Not only did the distinctive layout of alignments and avenues orchestrate the experience of the participants, defining its general character and determining its sequence, their very configuration involved a further element of stage-management. I mentioned the increasing size of the stones towards the western end of the Le Ménec alignment. This would have provided an increasing feeling of containment before the final enclosure was reached; to a lesser extent the same applies to its eastern terminal. Similar effects could be achieved by very simple means, but would have added materially to the experience of the participants. For example, in some of the shorter stone rows in the British Isles the heights of the uprights are graded in the same way as we saw in my Corsican examples. It was generally the tallest stone that was the only one to be decorated (Thom *et al* 1990, 387–90). This gains added significance when we realise that some of these stone rows followed basic astronomical alignments. I shall return to this point.

In the case of avenues leading towards monuments similar effects may have been important. As John Barrett suggests, the striking kink in the avenue leading into Avebury could have been intended to conceal the interior of the monument until the last possible moment (Barrett in press), and like other enclosures of this type, its bank was built on a larger scale on either side of the entrance, thus adding to the same effect. Inside Durrington Walls we find a similar phenomenon, and here the avenue of posts leading to the Southern Circle is blocked by a wooden facade (Wainwright & Longworth 1971, fig 17). We can also consider the Stonehenge avenue (RCHME 1979, 11–13). Its chronology is rather uncertain, but I am not convinced that it was built over a long period. It starts at the River Avon and runs for nearly 1.5 kilometres before Stonehenge can be seen at all. Then it extends for another 750 metres before its final change of direction. Only the last 500 metres of that earthwork (under 20% of its total length) were directed towards the entrance of the enclosure. The same effect is seen in some of the larger cursuses. In this case the banks that close off the ends of these monuments might be built on a much greater scale than the remainder of the earthwork, and on some sites no entrance was provided through this barrier. The increased scale of these terminals might

have had two effects. As we have seen already, they could have imitated the characteristic form of the long barrows found in the landscape around them, but they could also have closed off any view along the axis of these monuments from those not entitled to enter the interior: in that sense they were also a screen. On a far smaller scale, and probably at a later date, the ends of the Dartmoor stone rows could be provided with similar obstacles (Emmett 1979).

◆ ◆ ◆

An alignment not only determines the order in which information is provided; it also links places and phenomena that might otherwise exist in isolation. That isolation can be both geographical and intellectual. I can best illustrate this point by returning to a few sites that I have mentioned already. The Dorset Cursus links up a series of mortuary monuments that had originally been built in isolation, and probably over an appreciable period of time. Exactly the same applies to the Carnac alignments which also forge a link between hitherto independent mortuary monuments and menhirs. In some cases the time scale may have been rather longer. Not only does the surviving avenue at Avebury connect the Sanctuary to the main henge monument; it also connects a location with a very long history of human activity, Overton Hill, to a new construction where such evidence is largely lacking (Thomas, J 1991, 162–75). Francis Pryor goes even further in discussing the way in which the Maxey cursus connects the causewayed enclosure at Etton with a later henge. He suggests that this expresses the transfer of significance from one ceremonial site to another (Pryor in press). It creates a direct association between these separate places and the activities taking place there, and in doing so it also builds a link between the past and the present.

The same applies to two sites in the Stonehenge environs. The Greater Cursus runs from the edge of a zone above the River Avon associated with evidence of Earlier Neolithic settlement into another area in which we find the main concentration of long barrows (Richards, J 1990, 93-6). In this sense it joins the living to the dead. It also follows an alignment which might provide a powerful symbolism. Looking eastwards from the zone of mortuary monuments an observer would have seen the equinoctial sunrise over the opposite terminal of the cursus: that is to say, in the area associated with the settlements of the living. Six months later an observer in the settlement zone would see the sun set over the area reserved for monuments to the dead (illus 28). We can take a rather similar approach to the Stonehenge avenue, whatever its place in the sequence on that site. It joins this idiosyncratic enclosure to the Avon valley, where some of the largest henges had been built, and runs across a ridge which had formed the focus for a series of specialised deposits (*ibid*, 109–23). Along its route it also passes through a major cemetery. It emphasises the connection between phenomena of several different kinds and again it makes a link between the visible remains of different periods. Since so much of that activity left prominent earthwork monuments, it would be difficult to remain innocent of at least some of these associations. It is in this way, then, that monumental alignments of very different kinds may help to create a sense of timeless order. That synthesis may go against the archaeological evidence of sequence, but it lies at the heart of our conception of ritual.

On the other hand, there is a more detailed level of analysis at which it is not appropriate to consider all alignments in the same way. This is partly determined by chronology and geography, but it is also demanded by the details of their construction. I have already mentioned the increasing feeling of closure towards one end of the Carnac alignments, but the fact remains that this cannot be compared exactly with the sense of closure experienced inside the terminal of one of the larger cursuses. Some of the most massive alignments, such as those at Carnac or Avebury, are entirely permeable constructions (illus 29). At Avebury there is even a gap in one of the lines of uprights where the avenue crosses an earlier focus of activity (Smith 1965, 185–7). Such distinctions may have been important to those who built these monuments, and this could be why the earthwork avenue at Stonehenge apparently replaced an alignment of stones (Pitts 1984, 90–7).

◆ ◆ ◆

The implications of this contrast are important. A continuous earthwork barrier, such as the Dorset Cursus or the Stonehenge avenue, could not easily be breached. It made a very clear distinction between those who might be allowed inside the

28
Outline plan of the Stonehenge Cursus (after Richards, J 1990) emphasising the zones of domestic activity and funerary monuments towards its east and west terminals respectively.

monument and those who were excluded. Yet there is also some evidence for this distinction at Avebury where geophysical survey suggests that the greatest concentration of human traffic was along the outside of the West Kennet avenue (Ucko *et al* 1991, 186–94). Perhaps the creation of an earthwork at Stonehenge helped to formalise this distinction. At Le Ménec, on the other hand, the rather chaotic course of the outer stones of the alignment (Thom & Thom 1978, fig 6.3a) might be explained in another way (Julian Thomas pers comm). Could this arrangement have been intended to lead some of the participants **past** the great walled enclosure that forms the terminal cromlech? In that case the separate rows of stones would help to enforce a distinction between those who were permitted to enter the enclosure and those who were left outside.

The layout of alignments makes it easier to enforce distinctions of this kind. We have already seen some of the ways in which they can allow different levels of participation. This point is worth taking further. The most basic feature of any alignment, as distinct from a circular enclosure, is that it is long and narrow: everyone cannot move down it together. As John Barrett says, some people will have to go first, and others will be last. This is an important point as it provides a mechanism for grading the different participants (Barrett in press). The Dorset Cursus, for instance, is the largest earthwork of its kind. It may be 10 kilometres long but it is only 100 metres wide. There is an immediate contrast between the size of any group who could move along this earthwork together and the number of people required to build it in the first place. The Carnac alignments are of about the same

29
The Kermario alignment at Carnac, looking towards the west. Photograph: Aubrey Burl.

width, yet they run for four kilometres. The Stonehenge avenue is only 30 metres wide. Practical considerations dictate that if many people moved along them they would have had to form an orderly procession.

In fact some of these distinctions may have been significant even when the monuments were built. Indeed, that process could have helped to establish the power of these conventions. Again the evidence from Carnac is very revealing (illus 30). Detailed analysis of the ground-plan of the alignments shows that they consist of numerous short rows of stone, each of them of roughly the same size. They indicate a pattern of segmentary construction which is most unlikely to be the result of modern renovation, not least because this pattern was unrecognised until Alexander Thom undertook his detailed survey of the site (Thom & Thom 1978, ch 6, ch 7). Many of these short rows can be identified from slight idiosyncrasies in the alignment and spacing of the stones, as if each segment was the contribution of a single group, whose major limitation was the size of the largest stone that they could manoeuvre into place. There is only limited evidence for close control over this process. By contrast, we have seen how the alignments were constructed from much larger materials towards their terminals. The cromlechs that close them off have a far more regular ground-plan. Not only would this have required greater organisation, the physical labour of building the terminals must have entailed a larger labour force, working with more coordination. Similar distinctions can be seen in the fabric of cursuses. The side ditches were simple constructions, but a few of the earthwork terminals again made greater demands. In the case of the Dorset Cursus there is even the complicating factor that the long sides of the monument were built in different ways. One was a significant earthwork with a sharply cut ditch and a revetted bank. The other was rather slighter. It followed a more sinuous course and was interrupted by causeways of unexcavated chalk. The con-

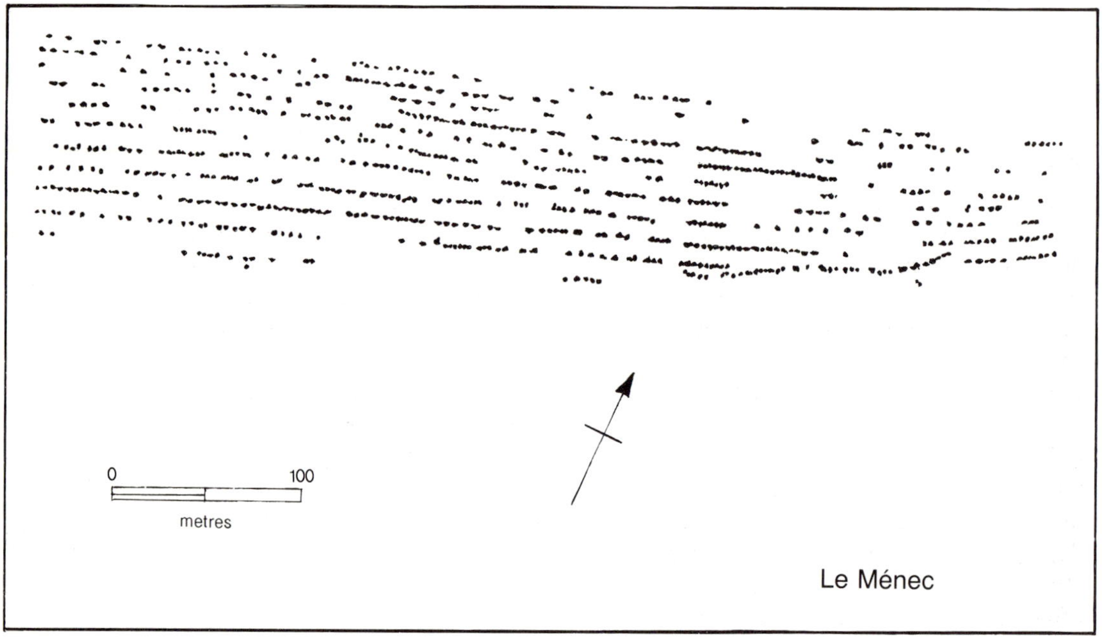

30
Detailed plan of part of the Le Ménec alignment at Carnac, emphasising its construction in short segments. (After Thom & Thom 1978).

0 ——— 100
metres

Le Ménec

trast has been noted at several locations, but the major earthwork is not always the same one; they seem to have changed places at least twice (Barrett *et al* 1991, 47). This may be related to the pattern of movement around the landscape as a whole. The intention could have been to locate the major barrier where it would confront more people.

Lastly, there is no reason to suppose that, once created, these monuments were left unchanged. There are numerous cases in which they might be refurbished or extended, but more revealing are those instances in which the building of a major alignment seems to have been re-enacted. The distinction is a subtle one, but it is most important. By repairing and renewing an existing alignment, the population expressed its continued commitment to the ideas that lay behind it – or, at least, to their own interpretation of them. This has been clearly documented at the Breton alignment of Saint-Just, where a sequence of stone rows, timber alignments, and a narrow cairn were all found at the same site. In this case their construction and use spanned hundreds of years (Le Roux *et al* 1989). At other sites entirely new alignments could be built. Some of these reinforced those patterns that had already been established, for example where a whole series of overlapping stone rows could be built across the same piece of ground (Emmett 1979; Thom *et al* 1990). A variant of this pattern has been identified at Maxey where the linear monument which we think of as a cursus may be no more than the aggregate of a succession of episodes of earthwork building, all on the same alignment. The Maxey cursus may never have been a unitary conception, visible on the ground at any one time (Pryor & French 1985, 301). It was essentially an idea, a project.

If many of these distinctions were inculcated from the moment that a monument was built, others could be emphasised during its operation. Cursuses can provide the focus for a series of structured deposits of artefacts, human remains and animal bones. Yet at some sites these may be found inside the enclosure and at others they are kept outside. For example, a series of fine artefacts were deposited in and around the Dorset Cursus, but it was only in the interior that elaborate lithic artefacts were found by excavation; material resulting from the preliminary processing of raw material was excluded (Barrett *et al* 1991, 70–5). Moreover, the ditch of this monument contained finds of human remains, accompanied by wild cattle bones. At other sites, such as the Drayton and Dorchester on Thames cursuses, unburnt human bones may be confined to the interior, with a particular emphasis on the head (Bradley & Chambers 1988, 284–6). By contrast, at Drayton pits containing Grooved Ware were limited to the exterior. There is too little evidence to take the argument any further, but this does raise the possibility that particular deposits were appropriate only in particular places. Given what I have said already about access to the interior, that also means that some people could provide these offerings, whilst others were prevented from doing so.

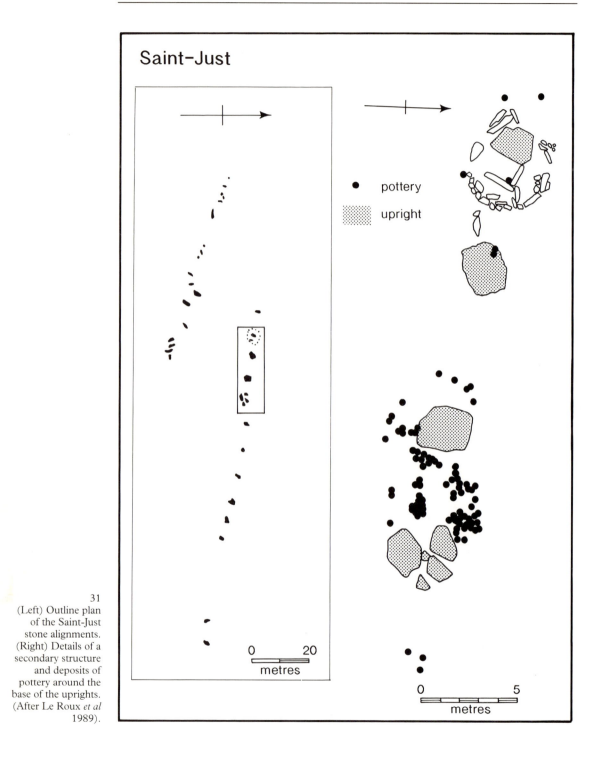

Saint-Just

pottery

upright

31
(Left) Outline plan
of the Saint-Just
stone alignments.
(Right) Details of a
secondary structure
and deposits of
pottery around the
base of the uprights.
(After Le Roux *et al*
1989).

0   20
metres

0   5
metres

That is not an isolated instance. In Brittany there is clear evidence that the stones in alignments and other settings formed the focus for rather similar deposits, sometimes accompanied by a stone-built hearth. Such evidence was recorded by early excavators at Carnac (Miln 1881), and at individual menhirs (Giot *et al* 1979, 398–9). It was also documented at the cromlech of Er Lannic (Le Rouzic 1930), but only recently has this kind of deposit been recorded in sufficient detail. Le Roux's excavation of the alignment of Saint-Just sheds fascinating light on the provision of offerings of this kind, associated with different phases in the use of a small alignment (Le Roux *et al* 1988; illus 31). Again, larger scale work is needed to determine whether particular kinds of material were appropriate in particular parts of these monuments: finds of pottery and axes are commonly mentioned in early accounts. I shall return to this question at the end of the lecture.

◆ ◆ ◆

We must also consider the relationship between alignments and the world around them. It is perhaps no accident that some of them were perpetuated in later patterns of land division. This applies particularly clearly to the two largest cursus complexes in England, the Dorset Cursus and those at Rudston on the Yorkshire Wolds, both of which were partially reused in a network of Iron Age territorial boundaries (Bowen 1990, 47–51; Dent 1982, fig 12). The fact is that these great alignments divide up large areas of the landscape. Although there is no evidence that they played a practical role in the demarcation of resources, they would certainly have formed an obstacle to free movement across the terrain. Other monuments may have had a similar impact, but on a much smaller scale. On Dartmoor, for instance, some of the existing stone rows were respected by the Bronze Age land divisions known as reaves, whilst other examples were slighted (Fleming 1988, ch 7). Similarly, in Brittany, where changes of sea level make the original topography more difficult to recreate, there is no doubt that some of the most massive stone alignments cross tracts of rather higher ground dividing up the landscape in very much the same fashion as territorial boundaries. Four such alignments go together to cut off the modern promontory at Carnac (Thom & Thom 1978, figs 9.3, 9.6), whilst two others cut across the Quiberon peninsula (Burl 1985, 164, 166). In Finistère another two complexes of this type cross the neck of land east of Camaret sur Mer (*ibid*, 66-8, 79). Even at a mundane level, the existence and operation of these monuments would have impinged on the pattern of movement around them.

In some cases those alignments would have had a more drastic effect on the ways in which the landscape was perceived. In north-west France there are cases in which alignments divide the landscape into a series of rectilinear units (*ibid*, 66–8). A comparable arrangement, but on a much larger scale, is found at Rudston on the Yorkshire Wolds, where four different cursuses intersect the Great Wold Valley, with the Rudston monolith at the centre of their distribution. Their use of the topography is remarkably like that of the Dorset Cursus, but in this case the juxtaposition of these four enormous monuments also has the effect of dividing up the terrain according to the cardinal points (Riley 1988, fig 5.1). Again, the symbolic dimension may be very important. The Dorset Cursus links a whole series of existing

mortuary monuments, but it also separates an upland area which was the main source of high quality flint from the main river valleys which are likely to have formed an important focus for settlement. In fact, some time after its first construction, it divided a series of extensive occupation sites involved in flint artefact production from a lowland area in which the main group of henge monuments was built (Barrett *et al* 1991, 59–70, 92–108; illus 32).

The Rudston complex had rather similar connotations. The cursuses found at this site establish a major north–south axis, breached by two shorter monuments of the same type and most likely of the same date. It is probable that all these were first

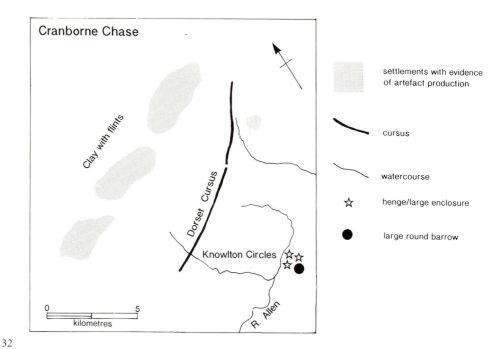

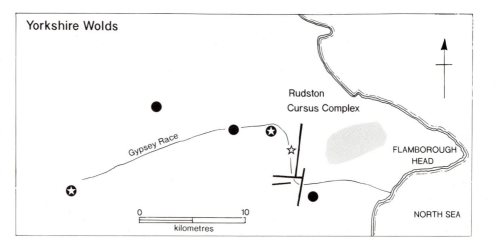

32
(Upper) The relationship of the Dorset Cursus to major henge monuments and the main settlement area with evidence of lithic production (after Barrett *et al* 1991). (Lower) The relationship of the Rudston cursuses to the distribution of major monuments (data from Manby 1988) and settlements producing elaborate flint artefacts (information from Tess Durden).

built during the Early Neolithic period, and, like the Dorset Cursus, one of these earthworks ends at an enlarged terminal which looks just like a long barrow. To the east of this axis were major sources of raw material along the beaches below Flamborough Head (Tess Durden pers comm), whilst all the long barrows of the Yorkshire Wolds were built to the west of this division. The distinction is perpetuated in the Late Neolithic. To the east of the Rudston complex were a number of settlement sites, the most important of which may have been making elaborate flint artefacts out of raw material introduced from the coastline (Tess Durden pers comm). To the west were all the Neolithic enclosures on the Wolds and all but one of the great round barrows of this region (Manby 1988). These mounds are especially important as they contain some of the specialised artefacts made on the other side of this alignment. Such distinctions may even be found at the local scale. Not far from Rudston is the Kilham long barrow (Manby 1976). At a developed stage in its construction its mound was approached by an avenue of paired posts. In one direction this led people to the monumental facade in front of the mortuary deposits. In the other, it was aligned in the general direction of the cursus complex. In this instance all trace of the posts had been destroyed not far from the barrow, but there are other cases in which the mound itself was lengthened during a secondary phase.

In certain cases the axis of major alignments almost certainly reflects basic astronomical events. This evidence will be familiar (Heggie 1981) but it is important for several reasons. I am unhappy with the argument that such alignments were instituted for the purposes of scientific observation, if only for the logical reason that the movements of the heavenly bodies would have to have been understood **before** these monuments were built. Again this involves a reference to the past, for such monuments clearly enshrine patterns that had already been observed. The choice of these orientations adds another dimension to certain monuments even if it is not their raison d'être.

A number of these alignments would only work in combination with natural features of the terrain, such features as mountains or passes. This is important because it forges yet another link between the creation and operation of monuments and the workings of the natural world. Some of the places that I discussed in my previous lecture may have had similar attributes. Menhirs could often have been used in combination with distant parts of the landscape to observe the movements of the sun and moon, but in this case those natural events have been annexed and brought into the world of human culture.

At the same time, I have placed some emphasis on the question of access. Some monuments were structured in such a way that not everyone would have been able to go inside them. Despite the size of the workforce involved in their construction, such sites were too small to have held many people. Moreover, these monuments were not self-explanatory. Even if the wrong people were able to find their way into a major cursus, they would need to know exactly where to position themselves if they were to understand its placing in the cultural landscape. Just as important,

in those admittedly rare cases in which cursuses had been laid out on the rising or setting sun, it would be essential to possess the further knowledge of when that event was to happen. The same argument applies to the other kinds of alignment. Their operation only makes complete sense under two conditions: the participants must know **where** to place themselves in order to appreciate the subtleties of the design, and they must know **when** to do so, otherwise the astronomical significance of those sites would be completely lost on them. In that respect they would be at much the same disadvantage as we are in investigating these sites today.

But taken another way, these observations could have a powerful impact. Those who built the monuments were able to link them to the most basic elements of the cosmos and at the same time to restrict the detailed knowledge of that relationship by constructing a monument in which there was space for only a limited number of observers. Astronomical events like the midwinter sunset on the Dorset Cursus, or the equinoctal sunrise on the Stonehenge Cursus, could only be seen from one carefully chosen position, and access to this might have been controlled (Barrett *et al* 1991, 58). Thus the restrictions that seem to be implicit in the very layout of certain monuments go beyond the question of access and unimpeded movement. They also extend to specialised knowledge: the knowledge of the basic alignments hidden in the design. This would not be accessible to outsiders, who could not have observed these phenomena. But at the same time, by controlling movement within such monuments, people might also have seemed to be controlling time itself. It is not that alignments of these kinds were necessary to establish a calendar. Rather, the important point is that by linking the operation of great monuments to the unchanging world of nature their builders were putting the significance of these constructions beyond any kind of challenge. The same phenomena could be observed year after year. Through the creation of monumental architecture, society confirmed its stable structure. And it was by linking concepts of place to those of time that monuments have had such a profound influence over human experience.

So far I have talked about one class of monument and tried to explain how it is that monumental architecture can help to create a view of the world. But that still leaves another topic to consider. I have commented on the ways in which monuments may be linked to the areas outside them: by creating obstacles to unimpeded movement about the landscape; by their integration with natural features of the terrain; and by their use of astronomical alignments. In each case we need to move beyond the enclosed space of the monument itself to discuss its wider setting. Having considered how places were transformed into monuments, and how monuments acted as places, I must say rather more about the links between these domains.

◆ ◆ ◆

I have emphasised the distinction between the wild and the domestic at several points so far. It played a part in my discussion of the origins of monuments in the first lecture. In the second, I emphasised the ways in which natural places were gradually assimilated into the pattern of monument building; and now I have stressed how monuments themselves had an impact on the landscape around them. But how pervasive was the contrast between the cultural world of the monument and the natural world outside it? Have I imposed an anthropological cliché on the evidence, or does further material exist which can allow us to investigate this relationship?

In order to make much progress, we need to isolate a phenomenon which is common to both these worlds. I have mentioned one already. In my last lecture I talked about the ways in which natural places might be embellished by rock carvings and even how fragments of those carvings could be taken away from their original locations and incorporated into monuments. In this lecture I referred briefly to the placing of decoration in some of the British stone rows. Here we have a suitable field for investigation.

I have already observed that the roots of Atlantic rock art seemed to be closely bound up in the decoration of Irish passage tombs. Although I hazarded the opinion that the more public art of the passage graves might have its origin in the carvings found on natural surfaces, its precise source matters less than the fact that the two groups were closely related to one another (Johnston 1989, 182–219). It is in the Boyne tombs that the practice of Neolithic rock carving reaches its fullest development, but even at its most elaborate this system has many points in common with the petroglyphs found in other locations. It also shares some of these motifs with portable artefacts, particularly carved stone balls and Grooved Ware.

33
Angular motifs in the passage tomb at Knowth.
(Photograph: George Eogan.)

The art of the Boyne Valley may be unusually ornate, but it follows a relatively simple set of rules. The principal sites are defined by longer passages than their counterparts elsewhere in Ireland and, in contrast to the decoration found in shallower structures, at Knowth, and to a lesser extent at Newgrange, there is a division between angular and curvilinear motifs (Shee Twohig 1981, 93–121; O' Kelly 1982, ch 13, ch 14; Eogan 1986, ch 7, ch 8. The angular motifs (illus 33) include such characteristic devices as the chevron; the curvilinear motifs (illus 34) include a variety of arcs, circles and spirals, many of which centre on a single cup-mark.

34
Curvilinear motifs in
the passage tomb at
Knowth.
(Photograph:
George Eogan).

There is no uniformity in the organisation of the carvings inside most passage tombs, and at sites like Loughcrew there is only limited evidence of careful composition (Thomas, J 1992). In the large tomb at Knowth in the Boyne Valley the situation is very different, and here the contrast between angular and curvilinear designs seems to be reflected in the organisation of the motifs. Curvilinear motifs may be found at the centre of the monument and also on the kerbstones, in particular those located around the entrances. Angular design elements tend to be found **inside** the monument. This distinction between interior and exterior is the one that I wish to explore.

This same distinction is echoed in a number of different fields. In Orkney, for example, the angular motifs of passage grave art are repeated in the designs found within the houses at Skara Brae, a site where curvilinear decoration is limited to a few sherds (Shee Twohig 1981, 238–9; Richards, C 1991). At Barnhouse angular designs are also present within the buildings, but curvilinear motifs are found on pottery (*ibid*, 28–9). Yet they also occur in other media in Orkney, most notably on the lintels of passage tombs (Shee Twohig 1981, 227–8; Sharples 1984). There are hints of a wider system of connections and contrasts.

We can take the argument even further. Where curvilinear designs are found in greatest numbers are on rock carvings located in isolated positions in the landscape. Here cup-marks and cup-and-ring-marks are very common indeed and angular designs are hardly known. In northern Britain there is evidence that these different phenomena may have been closely related to one another, and in Northumberland and Mid Argyll the most complex curvilinear designs are found on natural surfaces in the vicinity of Late Neolithic ceremonial sites (Bradley 1991). At the same time, the Grooved Ware found inside monuments of this kind is almost entirely limited to angular decoration.

So far there is little to bridge the gap between these two styles, but in fact such information is already to hand. In a recent paper Rosamund Cleal commented on the repeated discovery of vessels with complex Grooved Ware decoration in structured deposits at the entrance of henge monuments (1991, 141–5). On several sites this included the rare curvilinear decoration that has features in common with the motifs carved in stone. With one exception, sherds with this kind of decoration did not occur inside the same monuments. With that observation in mind, it is worth examining the relationship between enclosures and decorated stones. Although the evidence is of poor quality, it is actually rather revealing. Carvings are not common on stone circles, but those that do occur are usually simple cup-marks (Burl 1976). These are generally found on the exterior of the monument. Most examples are recorded from Recumbent Stone Circles, where these motifs are associated with the recumbent itself and with the uprights immediately flanking it (Ruggles & Burl 1985, 54–6). More complex motifs are uncommon but are exclusively curvilinear, and these are found in the same positions. Such motifs are more often found in the surrounding landscape but usually occur beyond the confines of the monuments themselves. The main exceptions are where outliers, rather than the stones of the circle, are associated with curvilinear motifs.

A good example illustration of this pattern comes from the Eden Valley in Cumbria (Beckensall 1992). The most famous site in this area is the large stone circle known as Long Meg and her Daughters. The uprights of the circle itself are entirely undecorated, but the one outlier is of a different raw material and is profusely carved with motifs found in passage tomb art. This stone is also located on the axis of the midwinter sunset, as viewed from the centre of the circle. Not far away are other monuments with carved decoration. The original form of these sites is not always clear, but both Glassonby and Little Meg include stones that were ornamented in the same style. They reveal an interesting contrast. At Little Meg the decorated stone faces outwards, whilst a stone in a similar position at Glassonby looks inwards towards the centre of the site. In this case the curvilinear designs are combined with chevron decoration.

We can also consider the decorated stone rows that I mentioned before. The carved motifs are generally confined to the shorter rows and are usually discovered at the end of the alignment, on the tallest upright; again cup-marks are the most common element (Thom *et al* 1990, 387–90). These sites share a further feature with other groups of decorated monument, for in each case individual examples follow basic astronomical alignments. From the point of view of the audience utilising those sites there is one common element, for in such cases the decorated stones **face outwards**. They are located at the point at which that alignment extends into the wider landscape, and it is of course in that landscape that more elaborate curvilinear motifs are found.

So this emphasis on curvilinear designs is shared between different kinds of monument and also between different media. It is illustrated by the deposition of decorated pottery, but it is equally apparent from the decoration applied to stone circles, and particularly to outlying stones. It reflects the basic principles according to which passage grave art was organised at Knowth, with curvilinear decoration looking out into the landscape and angular motifs more frequent in the internal area of the monument. As we have seen, this emphasis on angular motifs is repeat-

ed in the decoration of the houses at Skara Brae. The presence of reused stones bearing angular designs among the finds from Bronze Age barrows shows that these motifs once had a wider distribution (Bradley 1992). Following these observations, we might be seeing some reflection of a broader distinction between the cultural area of the monument and the natural world beyond it. That would certainly account for the distinctive locations at which the more complex open air carvings are found.

If I confined my argument to rock carvings, it would not be at all convincing. Too few stone monuments were decorated, and too few other monuments have been excavated with the distribution of decorated pottery in mind. But in fact this contrast is echoed in several different media. The curvilinear designs on the pottery deposited at the entrance of henge monuments tend to be associated with other classes of material culture. In particular, one artefact type which featured in a previous lecture is worth considering here.

◆ ◆ ◆

There has been considerable discussion of the relationship between henges and the movement of polished axes, and it is certainly true that these objects are clustered in areas with these monuments. But at a more detailed level, finds of axes show the same general pattern as pottery with curvilinear decoration; that is to say, they are mainly in the entrance to these monuments or the entrances to the timber circles found within their interior (Bradley & Edmonds in press; illus 35). In other cases they are confined to the perimeter earthwork. Far more axes may be discovered outside these enclosures, where they may sometimes form part of complex pit deposits containing other non-local artefacts. By contrast, different kinds of lithic artefact are discovered inside these monuments.

This distinction echoes another contrast that was identified some time ago: the deposits found inside

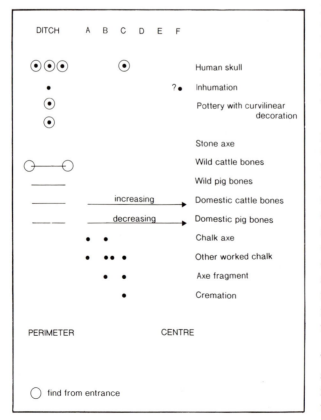

35
The location of different classes of excavated material in relation to the post circles and perimeter earthwork at Woodhenge. For the plan of a very similar structure see illus 56 (Mount Pleasant).

DITCH   A   B   C   D   E   F

Human skull
Inhumation
Pottery with curvilinear decoration
Stone axe
Wild cattle bones
Wild pig bones
increasing   Domestic cattle bones
decreasing   Domestic pig bones
Chalk axe
Other worked chalk
Axe fragment
Cremation

PERIMETER   CENTRE

○ find from entrance

henges tend to be associated with domestic animal bones, whilst wild animals are much better represented around the perimeter (Thomas, J 1991, 70–3). We can add a little detail to that contrast for it is also illustrated by the finds of antler at these sites. At Durrington Walls nearly all the antler picks were in very large deposits close to the entrance of the site and also in the post holes by the entrance to the Southern Circle (Wainwright & Longworth 1971). Red deer skulls and unused antler follow the same distribution on excavated sites, suggesting that the pattern is not entirely the result of how their construction was organised (cf Barrett *et al* 1991, table 3.12).

Do any other deposits show this distinctive patterning? I would suggest two further examples. The relatively rare carved chalk objects found in southern English henges also tend to be associated with the entrances to these sites, the perimeter and even the area outside. Their interpretation is problematical, but they certainly include some objects that might indicate a concern with fertility. Lastly, even the human remains from henges show a certain patterning. Most stratified cremations come from the edges of these sites or the internal area, whilst unburnt human bones, generally in the form of weathered fragments, are found at the entrance, or elsewhere on the boundary. Skull fragments are most often recognised in these locations. The distinction might be that between the complex cultural treatment of the body – its cremation on a pyre – and the processes of natural decay that could have been associated with the wild. Indeed, there could be links between some of these separate categories of material. For instance, we might compare the finds of antler with those of isolated human bones. Aubrey Burl even suggests that the cyclical growth and shedding of antlers might symbolise a broader pattern of death and regeneration (1991, 34). A rather similar cycle is indicated where monuments were orientated on yearly astronomical events.

I have emphasised the evidence of specialised monuments, but in a number of cases the kinds of deposit that I associated with the entrances and boundaries of these sites are of types that are also found in pit deposits in the landscape as a whole. If that is true, it means that the deposition of a range of significant items was attended by the same basic rules, both inside these monuments and also in the landscape beyond them. They form part of a single system, but it is one that point-edly emphasises the contrast between the cultural world and the wild. It takes in house decoration at one extreme and the embellishment of impressive natural places at the other, and it seems to show that an interest in the boundaries between them was among the main concerns of Neolithic society. That is my justification for saying that the relationship between those two worlds was one that monument building helped to regulate.

Now we have seen a little of how monuments might have helped to inculcate a new sense of place. We have observed how natural places can be turned into monu-ments and even how some of their physical manifestations – sculptures or frag-ments of rock carvings – could be translated into a new, more monumental setting. We have also seen how those formal constructions influenced human perception and experience and how active a part they could play in the expression of social distinctions. That is how monuments work as **places**. Yet at the same time, the

exclusive character of those constructions needed constant protection and was reinforced by a distinctive symbolism and by the use and deposition of specific kinds of material. Certain people were excluded from these places, and so were certain elements of material culture. The distinction between insiders and outsiders echoes the geographical contrast between the private arena of the monument and the natural world round about it. In this sense the places that archaeologists call monuments were kept apart from other significant locations in the landscape.

I have said very much less about **time**, but the close integration between certain monuments and astronomical events can hardly be coincidental. Important as these were in the lives of farming people, it seems extremely unlikely that this was their main reason for existing. I prefer the argument proposed at the start of these lectures: that farming did not lead to the creation of monuments, or, indeed, monuments to farming. What monument building did achieve, but without any conscious planning, was a perception of the world that made agriculture easier to imagine and easier to execute. But the correct interpretation of those monuments would have been contentious from the moment of their creation, and for that reason they acquired a history that was unstable yet very distinctive. My second group of lectures move on from place to time as they attempt to follow that sequence.

4

MONUMENTS AS IDEAS

Monuments are not only places in which human experience was moulded in special ways. They are also the embodiment of ideas about the world. As such they can be adapted and changed from one period or area to another. This lecture considers how the stereotyped lay-out of Neolithic enclosures was adopted and modified by communities in a variety of cultural settings, from Central Europe to Scandinavia and Western France. The changing history of this type of earthwork epitomises the way in which a particular form of monument can stand for a wider view of human experience.

◆ ◆ ◆

When prehistoric artefacts were exchanged, they carried their past histories with them. When archaeologists begin a new project, they bear a similar burden, and whether they intend it or not, their perspectives are always coloured by their earlier research.

Consider again the archaeology of Mid Argyll. I went there to visit the monuments, but it was not very long before I found myself thinking about the ways in which they might have been involved in the movement of portable artefacts. The west coast of Scotland contains a significant number of stone axes made in the Lake District mountains where I had worked for three years, yet in Argyll we also find axes that were brought across the Irish Sea (Sheridan 1986). That is no problem from a Scottish point of view – in other periods there are obvious links between Ulster and Argyll – but in fact the Irish axes were less suitable as work tools than their Cumbrian counterparts, and less suitable again than some of those made at Killin (Bradley *et al* 1992). When we recognise that Cumbrian axes were also crossing the Irish Sea, we learn something unexpected about the character of exchange systems in prehistory.

I thought along these lines as I considered one of the main monuments on the west coast of Scotland, the remarkable complex at Temple Wood, for in one phase of its history two of the upright stones were inscribed with motifs that are normally found in Irish megalithic art (Scott 1989, 105–6; illus 36). The reference seems obvious enough, but like the distribution of stone axes, it forces us to think rather harder about the movement of ideas. The distribution of stone axes makes little 'economic' sense; it expresses a purely cultural link. The sharing of certain symbols reflects the same priorities.

Now let me add a third element to this account. At certain stages in its development Temple Wood was a freestanding enclosure, the end product of a very long history of Neolithic enclosures in Britain (illus 37). Some of the oldest examples are strongly implicated in the dissemination of stone axes. The distribution of those sites was once confined to England, but it keeps expanding. A causewayed enclosure has been discovered in Ulster (Mallory & Hartwell 1984) and there is now one on Anglesey (Mark Edmonds & Julian Thomas pers comm). Roger Mercer has suggested a possible example in Kintyre (1981, 195), and thermoluminescence dating even raises the possibility that a vitrified fort in Grampian is of Neolithic date (Strickertsson *et al* 1988). There is a sense in which these processes – the circulation of imported artefacts, the deployment of foreign symbols and the adoption of exotic types of monument – all have features in common.

36
Upright with spiral decoration in the Temple Wood stone circle, Argyll. Photograph: Historic Scotland.

They are not the result of migration or simply of 'trade': they relate to the use of material culture as a vehicle for the expression of ideas. In this lecture I shall try to explore that notion in more detail by tracing the history of one kind of monument.

I have elected to talk about monuments as ideas. But whose ideas are they to be? So far they have been those of archaeologists. I have talked about how monuments influence human conduct. They change people's experience of time and place, and in certain instances they form links between their day to day activities and the workings of nature. Although that takes us beyond monument typology, it remains very much an outsider's view, for it discounts the perspective of the participants. In this lecture, and the lecture that follows it, I would like to redress the balance, extending the argument from individual monuments to ceremonial centres. First, I shall work at a large geographical scale, tracing the history of a single class of monument in Britain and Continental Europe and the changes that took place as its distribution extended from one cultural setting to another. Then, in the following lecture, I shall sharpen the focus, discussing how individual monuments and complexes of monuments in the British Isles were adapted and changed over time.

◆ ◆ ◆

Archaeologists see monuments as types, but for those who built them they would have been the embodiment of ideas, in the same way as the cruciform plan of a Christian church is both architecture and theology combined. But just as beliefs

37
General view of the Temple Wood stone circle, Argyll. Photograph: Historic Scotland.

can be modified and reassessed, there is nothing that is fixed about the forms of early monuments, and it is this that makes them so difficult to classify. As a visible embodiment of ideas about the world, they are rarely absent from human consciousness, and when those ideas are modified we should expect the new interpretations to be echoed in subtle ways by the changing configuration of those monuments or the changing ways in which they were used (Thomas, J 1991, ch 3). That is surely the premise of a contextual archaeology. So far the patterns I have described have not been particularly subtle ones. For example, the links between long houses and megaliths are conceived at a very broad level, as we might expect when their distributions overlap to such a limited extent. I shall consider a type of monument which is found with both settlements and tombs. To what extent does the changing character of Neolithic **enclosures** echo the broader distinctions that I outlined in my first lecture?

Why are enclosures so well suited to this kind of discussion? They have a wide distribution, from Central Europe to France, and from Ireland to Scandinavia. They have a long chronology, from the Linearbandkeramik to the TRB, and yet they share an unusually stereotyped ground-plan. As we shall see, many of them also contain a series of rather similar deposits. Yet at the same time, these enclosures embody a whole series of contrasts that may shed light on the changing character of Neolithic society. Before I consider in any detail how such enclosures developed, I should say something about the sheer variety that they encompass. But these are simply the broad outlines, for few sites are entirely alike.

There are several dimensions to consider, and I shall mention the most important now. First of all, we can distinguish between those enclosures found in areas with a long history of hunting and gathering and monuments found in regions in which agricultural colonisation is well-attested. If megalithic tombs were mainly a feature of the agricultural margin, enclosures first developed at its core, on the loess soils of West Central Europe (Lüning 1988; illus 38). In some areas enclosures may be closely integrated with settlements, whilst in others they are entirely separate from them. And where settlements are clearly evidenced, they may be preceded by the construction of enclosures, or the enclosures can develop at a later stage, alongside the settlement itself or even after its abandonment. At the same time, the history of causewayed enclosures extends beyond the edges of the loess into areas of Neolithic Europe in which domestic sites are less apparent. Again this may also be reflected by changes in the character of the monuments.

Secondly, the form of the enclosures could also be subject to modification. There are some examples with very formal ground-plans and others which lack this characteristic entirely. Their sizes vary considerably and so do their histories of use. Individual sites may have functioned over a very short period, whilst others were constructed with a view to careful maintenance and could have been modified and renewed for a long time. In some cases these changes involved a novel role for certain of the enclosures, so that a small number of earthworks assumed a defensive character. In certain instances the development of defended sites may have been connected with control over particular resources or even with their role in craft production.

Alternatively, individual enclosures may have been more closely integrated into ritual and ceremonial. For example, we can recognise changes in their relationship with flat cemeteries, mounds and cairns. This even extends to the discovery of human remains in both groups. At the same time, particular enclosures may also have become a focus for the deposition of cultural material, including elaborate or non-local artefacts, meat waste and the burials of domesticated animals. There are obvious contrasts in the scale and formality of such deposits from one site and one period to another, and we must ask whether similar deposits are known in other kinds of context.

Lastly, still further contrasts involve the later history of these sites. When and why did particular enclosures go out of use, and, as they did so, were the sites deserted or were they used in different ways? All these are themes that can be traced at a large geographical scale. Taken together, they illustrate the manner in which a single idea – that of enclosing a special area by an interrupted ditch – was deployed from one cultural setting to another. The process would normally be described as diffusion, but that is the kind of neutral terminology that archaeologists use to distance themselves from their subject matter. As I suggested earlier, **interpretation** is

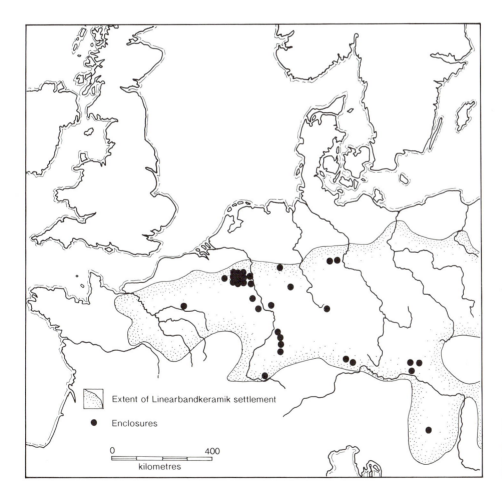

Extent of Linearbandkeramik settlement

● Enclosures

0   400
kilometres

38
The distribution of Linearbandkeramik enclosures (after Lüning 1988).

a more satisfactory term for this process. People drew on the history and associations of particular forms of monuments and they changed them in accordance with their needs and the character of their own society. I shall illustrate this point by showing how one 'type' of monument, as we call it, was transformed by different human groups across space and time, and the distinctive ways in which it was assimilated to their cultural conventions. We shall follow the causewayed enclosure across **space**, from the agricultural core to its periphery, and we shall trace its history through **time** from the exploitation of the loess to the broad spectrum economies of the agricultural margin. In doing so we shall move away from a Neolithic which is defined by its subsistence economy to one which is much better characterised by monuments: a Neolithic that is more securely based on cultural practice.

◆◆◆

The point of origin is obscure, but it lies within the late Linearbandkeramik (Lüning 1988). A number of trends come together here. By this stage, individual settlements had been in existence for a considerable length of time but had grown to varying extents. There is little evidence for major contrasts between these sites, yet it does appear that the production and distribution of certain artefacts and raw materials may have been focused at particular locations. Sometimes one house may be associated with the richest range of material culture (Lüning 1982). It does not seem likely that each individual settlement was accompanied by a cemetery, yet the burial record provides evidence of social differentiation (Whittle 1988, 150–64). The earliest enclosures are found in association with some but not all of the settlement clusters, although they also occur in more isolated positions.

At the regional scale it is clear that these enclosures are not uniformly distributed. They tend to be found towards the edges of Linearbandkeramik expansion, close to the limits of the loess (Lüning 1988). That is certainly consistent with their chronological position which suggests that they did not develop until a late phase of that culture. In some cases the enclosures may even have developed in a border area between the regions used by agriculturalists and the territories of contemporary hunter-gatherers (Keeley 1992).

Although quite a number of enclosures have been investigated, the oldest examples are poorly understood. Most sites have several entrances, yet only a minority of the Linearbandkeramik earthworks have the system of regularly placed causeways so familiar on later sites (Boelicke *et al* 1988, 417–28). The enclosures tend to be quite small, and there have been claims that they were built to a standard plan and even to standard sizes (Van Berg 1991). Their relationship to the settlement sites is really rather volatile. In a few instances there seems to be good evidence that the enclosed area contained houses, but there are certainly others in which the settlement phase is later than the creation of the enclosure (Boelicke *et al* 1988, 424–6). Sometimes the relationship between the settlements and enclosures is far less straightforward. At Langweiler 8 the excavators offer two alternative sequences (*ibid*). In the first scenario the settlement shifted through time towards the area where the enclosure was to be constructed. In this version the earthwork was built

alongside the last of the houses. In their other version the basic configuration of the settlement remains the same, but the enclosure was not built until all these houses had gone out of use. That sequence has more in common with the evidence from Langweiler 9 where two groups of domestic buildings were identified, separated by an area of open ground (Kuper *et al* 1977). In this case the enclosure was built in the unoccupied space, but only after both house clusters had been abandoned.

How are we to understand these relationships? Perhaps those two sites provide an important clue, for in each case the enclosure seems to have been constructed at the very end of the archaeological sequence, but in a space which had been kept clear of buildings for a long time. There may even be a relationship between the scale of the enclosures and the history of the earlier settlement. Thus Langweiler 8 was the longest lived and also the largest of the settlements of the Merzbach Valley, and Lüning (1982) suggests that it may have played an important role in the distribution of flint to sites in the surrounding area. Site 9, on the other hand, had a shorter history and was replaced by a less impressive earthwork.

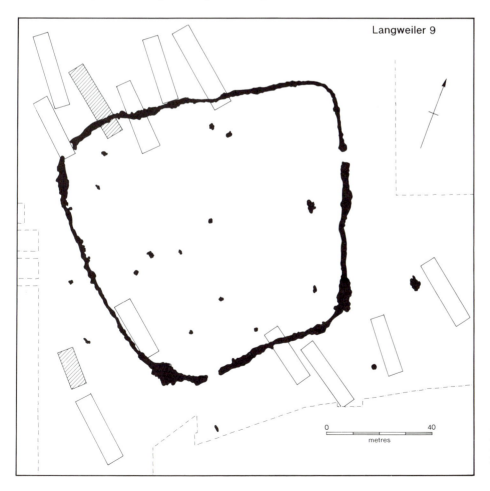

39
Outline plan of the earthwork enclosure and contemporary pits at Langweiler Site 9 (after Kuper *et al* 1977). The positions of earlier houses are shown in outline, and the latest of these are shaded.

In each case excavation supplies important clues. In some ways the less elaborate enclosure at Langweiler 9 is the more informative (Kuper *et al* 1977; illus 39). This earthwork cut across the ends of two earlier houses but otherwise it occupied an empty space within the settlement area. The only features inside the enclosure were pits, and there were a few more outside. The excavators have used the ceramic sequence on the site to reconstruct the pattern of movement around the settlement. This suggests that the enclosure was located in what had been the focal area in between two clusters of buildings. Its main characteristic was that it contained a concentration of the worked flint imported to the site. It may be that this was one area where communal activities took place and where tool production was concentrated.

If so, that activity continued and even intensified during the enclosure phase, when more worked flint was deposited in pits in the interior. There is also evidence for the deposition of two distinct tool kits in the pits belonging to the settlement. One was apparently connected with artefact production and the other with the preparation of food. Two of the pits underlying the enclosure contained assemblages of this kind, but after the earthwork had been built we encounter a more focused distribution of activities. Six pits contemporary with the enclosure contained flint assemblages associated with food preparation. There was also a major deposit of burnt flints towards the centre of the earthwork, possibly resulting from cooking. At the same time, the enclosure contained one of the pit groups linked with tool production. There is more limited spatial patterning among the finds from the ditch. Most of the pottery was concentrated towards the entrances, where it was associated with evidence of burning, but different ceramic forms had rather different distributions around the site.

Much less is known about the development of the enclosure at Langweiler 8, although this was a more complex structure, with no fewer than three concentric earthworks (Boelicke *et al* 1988). Again it developed in an area devoid of houses alongside the outer edge of the settlement, but in fact most of the excavated material came from one of the entrances facing away from the rest of the site. This included a concentration of quern fragments, and pieces of imported flint from three distinct sources. This is particularly interesting since it seems as if the earlier settlement had controlled the distribution of raw material to the other sites in the vicinity. Perhaps the enclosure played some part in the same process during the last use of the settlement, or even after occupation had ceased.

In each case it looks as if the enclosures were carefully located in an empty space within or alongside the settlement. They may have provided a focus for some of the more specialised activities that had already been established during earlier phases of occupation. On Site 8 these may have included the distribution of imported flint, whilst there is stronger evidence from Langweiler Site 9 that the enclosure was used for food preparation after the settlement itself had been abandoned. There is also a suggestion that the earthwork at Langweiler Site 9 lent greater emphasis to a prescribed space in the heart of the occupied area where houses had never been built. Rather the same impression is provided by the evidence from some of the enclosed settlement sites, in particular the causewayed

enclosure at Darion (Keeley & Cahen 1989) and the later palisaded site at Inden (Kuper & Piepers 1966), where the houses are located towards the outer perimeter, leaving most of the interior free of buildings.

The interlocking of settlements and enclosures is also illustrated by the Linearbandkeramik site at Sittard, where the remains of two segmented enclosures were found, together with a large number of house plans (Modderman 1959). The relationships between the enclosures and these houses are difficult to work out, but suggest a complicated horizontal stratigraphy (illus 40). In this case one of the enclosures was probably the earliest feature on the site, although it may have surrounded a group of long houses. At all events the settlement area eventually extended across the limits of that enclosure and several lengths of earthwork were cut by the borrow pits associated with new buildings on the site. A second enclosure seems to have been built against the position of the first one, but in this case the sequence was reversed, and in places the perimeter earthwork respected the positions of existing houses. Still more buildings were discovered outside the

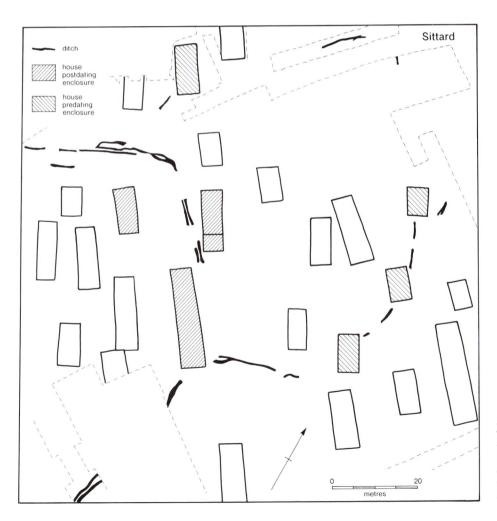

40
The relationship of the buildings at Sittard to the two enclosures on the site. (Data from Modderman 1958).

41
(Left) Outline
plans of the
ditched and/or
palisaded
enclosures of
Urmitz (phase 1)
and Noyen-sur-
Seine (phase 2).
(After Boelicke
1976 and Mordant
& Mordant 1977
respectively.)
(Right) Details of
the structures
associated with the
ditch terminals at
Caldern and
Sarup (phase 2).
(After Raetzel-
Fabian 1991 and
Andersen 1988
respectively.)

enclosure altogether. The pottery from the excavation belongs to at least two separate phases and its distribution emphasises some of these distinctions. One group is practically confined to the area delimited by the enclosures and the other is found outside them. Whatever the relationship between the first enclosure and the houses, it seems as if the final phase of the settlement was restricted to the area beyond these earthworks. If so, the sequence may be rather like that suggested at Langweiler 8, with the last houses of the settlement built alongside an enclosure.

The two enclosures at Sittard are very slight constructions, but by the end of the Linearbandkeramik some of the earthworks were becoming more elaborate. This is the first of our major transformations. Three developments are found more widely. The shape of the ditches often changed from a V profile to a flat-bottomed earthwork that would be easier to maintain over a long period (Whittle 1977). At the same time, more of the enclosure ditches were broken at regular intervals by causeways. This might be explained in practical terms, by the way in which earthwork construction was organised; as many people have pointed out, there is no need to

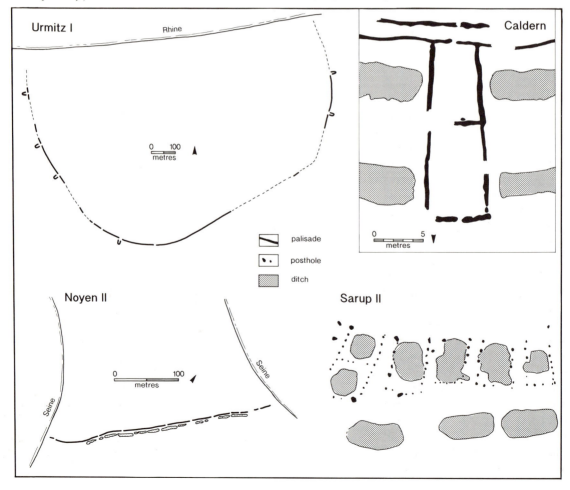

dig a continuous ditch in order to build a continuous bank. Although this argument may apply to later sites in the British Isles, it is quite unhelpful here, for at a number of enclosures on the Continent the segmented ditch was accompanied by an interrupted palisade (illus 41). Clearly the causeways were integral to the basic design.

The third feature is not so clearly documented. This is the claim that some of the enclosures were defended settlements. This view has been championed particularly strongly for late Linearbandkeramik sites in Belgium (Keeley & Cahen 1989). Although there are signs of quite long lengths of palisade, the argument is weakened by the numerous gaps in the ditches. There is certainly evidence that a number of the houses at these sites had been destroyed by fire, but sometimes that had happened before any earthworks were built. One feature that links the Belgian sites with those on the Aldenhoven Platte is the evidence for craft production. At Darion it seems that flint blades were being made for exchange, whilst the contemporary enclosure at Oleye contained a workshop producing fine pottery (*ibid*). A better known example of the same process is found at Spiennes where a rather later enclosure, defined by continuous ditches, was built beside the famous flint mines. The ditches were filled with debitage of the same character as the material found in the mine shafts (Scollar 1959; Hubert 1971).

◆ ◆ ◆

At this point we should pause. By the end of the Linearbandkeramik nearly all the characteristic features of Neolithic enclosures were in place. There was still a considerable diversity. Some enclosures had interrupted ditches and at other sites they were continuous. Certain enclosures contained settlements, but elsewhere they were found beyond the distribution of houses, or even in isolation. On some sites the enclosures were later than all the houses, whilst there were other earthworks where settlements developed after the enclosures had been built. Even so, the general pattern is clear. The enclosures were integrated into a long established agricultural landscape and sometimes formalised a pattern of activity that had already emerged during the occupation of the open settlements. Certain functions such as lithic production, the exchange of raw materials, food preparation and pottery manufacture were provided with an added significance. At the same time a small number of settlements were contained by earthworks of defensible proportions. It seems easy to suggest that this shows the growth of certain occupation sites at the expense of their neighbours, but the actual sequence is more complicated and some sites were only selected as settlements after their creation as monuments. A good example of this development is the classic site of Köln-Lindenthal (Buttler & Haberey 1936), where the excavators recognised a whole sequence of successive earthworks (illus 42). Although the area was settled on quite a large scale, the one enclosure with a segmented ditch does not seem to have been associated with any of the houses. It was succeeded by a larger earthwork which did contain a number of domestic buildings, and in this case the ditch formed a major barrier. It was deeper than its predecessors and was dug as a continuous earthwork.

How can we account for these developments? It seems almost as if particular groups may have been appropriating specialised monuments for their use and on occasion may have imposed a substantial barrier between themselves and the world outside. There are cases in which that development involved a change in the character of the earthworks, but in other instances these sites seem to have retained their segmented ground-plan. I mentioned that these developments continued after the Linearbandkeramik. This is significant in itself for it means that the characteristic enclosures went on in use into a period in which Neolithic culture became less uniform and we find a series of a smaller local groups.

The legacy of the Linearbandkeramik was varied and I cannot follow all the strands in one lecture. In Central Europe, for example, the enclosures were gradually transformed into a series of earthworks with an even more stereotyped ground-plan (Trnka 1991). This particularly emphasised the entrances to these sites, which were sometimes aligned on cardinal points or on astronomical events. These small enclosures were certainly not settlements, although houses have again been found outside them. The earthworks can be associated with finds of figurines and even with human remains. They represent one very special elaboration of the principle of the causewayed enclosure, but with a much greater emphasis on the depth and orientation of the various entrances. Ditches seem to be interchangeable with circuits of posts, and in their latest manifestation these sites have been compared with British henges. It would be intriguing to consider this suggestion here, but the lecture has a wide enough brief already, and I must confine myself to developments in north-west Europe.

In that area the segmented plan of the causewayed enclosure was carefully maintained. Indeed, it became so widespread that after its first appearance late in the Linearbandkeramik it became a remarkably standardised type of monument. By the Michels-

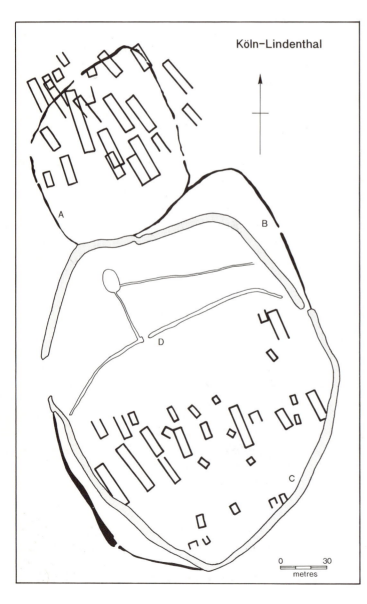

42
Outline plans of the houses and ditched enclosures at Köln-Lindenthal (after Buttler & Haberey 1936). The main features considered in the text are enclosures A and C.

Köln-Lindenthal

0   30
metres

berg phase it took much the same form over an enormous area from southern Germany to northern France. There are related examples as far south as Languedoc (Vaquer 1990, 294–6). We can recognise a few of the key points in the adoption of this kind of monument, but we cannot consider their entire distribution. In Germany itself it is some time before we find evidence for significant changes. The enclosures of the succeeding phases show much the same range of variation as their predecessors and the same interplay between earthwork monuments and settlements. In this case it was only in the Michelsberg phase that radically new developments arose. As we shall see, this coincides with the break-up of the long established pattern of settlement and with the apparent disappearance of cemeteries.

In northern France there is evidence of rather similar changes. There are late Linearbandkeramik cemeteries, but none of the Rössen period. The oldest enclosure, at Menneville in the Aisne Valley, belongs to this transitional phase (Coudart & Demoule 1982). This was apparently an enclosed settlement, and like the Belgian examples I mentioned before, it had an interrupted ditch. It was transitional in other ways too. Its use as a settlement site links it with earlier developments, but the causewayed earthwork around it anticipates the form of later monuments in northern France. The complex sequence of filling and recutting in this ditch contrasts with the normal pattern on Linearbandkeramik sites, where the earthworks rarely formed a focus for complex deposits. Among the finds from Menneville were articulated animal bones, and these are another feature that was to characterise later enclosures. In the same context were two child burials, and these occupy a transitional point in the sequence in still another way. The deposition of human remains in causewayed enclosures became a very widespread practice during later phases, but these burials were covered by red ochre, a feature that connects them with the late Linearbandkeramik cemeteries in the same area.

◆ ◆ ◆

With the end of the long house settlements on the loess, there is much less evidence for a regular association between enclosures and settlements. Obvious exceptions can still be found: at the famous site of Urmitz, for example, the first houses were built in the Michelsberg phase, some time after the enclosure itself had been created, and in this case those buildings were by no means substantial (Boelicke 1976). Another transitional site is Bery au Bac in the Aisne Valley where a group of Late Rössen houses were enclosed by a continuous earthwork (Dubouloz et al 1982), but such sites are really the exceptions that prove the rule, for at a more general level the relationship between settlement sites and enclosures seems to have been significantly weaker. This is particularly true of the Michelsberg phase.

Even where houses have been recognised inside enclosures of that date, the sites would seem to have assumed a range of additional functions. For some time it has been recognised that with the end of formal cemeteries there were new developments in the treatment of the dead, and often human bones have been discovered

by chance in ditches and other features. Indeed, at the type-site of Michelsberg itself, a considerable earthwork seems to have enclosed a series of pits containing human remains (Lüning 1967, 113–19, 297–332). That also extends to some of the enclosed settlements. At a recently excavated site in Belgium, a ditched and palisaded enclosure dated to the early Michelsberg produced evidence of small timber houses, but these were found together with a series of pits filled with burnt deposits and a grave containing a child's skull (Veermeersch & Walter 1980). The Michelsberg enclosed settlement at Mairy in the Ardennes reveals an equally complicated situation (Marolle 1989). This contained an unusual range of large houses but at the same time the excavator also identified a series of distinctive pit deposits. These had a complex filling and included articulated animal bones, elaborate artefacts and complete pots (illus 43). There seems little doubt that this material had been deposited with considerable formality, and for that reason it is unlikely that these pits were simply for storing food.

Similar changes took place at defended sites, and here again we find an individual mixture of the sacred and profane. A number of enclosures in northern France had considerable earthworks including substantial stone-walled ramparts. Similar sites are also found in the east of the country. Some of the examples recognised in the Paris Basin had been burnt and their ramparts had been demolished. This had happened at Boury where the remains of the levelled stonework were overlain by a remarkable series of animal burials, ranged symmetrically on either side of a causeway in the ditch (Lombardo *et al* 1984). These may well have been the remains of sacrifices, and the sheer scale of this deposit outstrips any similar examples so far found in northern France. At a later date the animal burials were sealed by a level of fragmentary human remains. Although the excavation was on a limited scale, the site shows very clearly how misleading it is to distinguish between the utilitarian and ritual use of these

43
Sections of
selected pits in
the Michelsberg
enclosure at
Mairy (after
Marolle 1989).

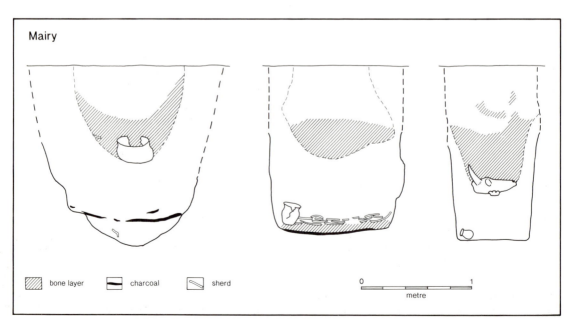

Mairy

bone layer   charcoal   sherd

0   1
metre

locations; the enclosure had quite possibly been attacked and destroyed, yet one of the causeways in its ditch formed the focus for a series of lavish offerings.

━━━━━━━━━ ◆◆◆ ━━━━━━━━━

Again it is worth taking stock. The evidence of these sites suggests that after the late Linearbandkeramik the idea of building enclosures was adopted widely. In Central Europe, the main emphasis was on the construction of numerous entrances, a feature that was surely inspired by prototypes among the causewayed enclosures. It was in this area that these earthworks assumed their greatest formality, and this was matched by the deposition of specialised material within these sites. These were certainly not settlements, although houses might be built near to them.

Elsewhere the sequence of change was less abrupt. Although causewayed enclosures were constructed in increasing numbers, this did not displace the alternative practice of creating continuous earthworks, and both could be associated with settlements. On the other hand, it is in those areas at the edge of the Linearbandkeramik expansion that we find the clearest evidence of new developments. To a large extent these ran in parallel with the demise of individual burial in cemeteries and with the break-up of a settlement pattern characterised by groups of long houses. Where enclosures continued to be inhabited there seems to be evidence for new kinds of practices. The earthworks can be laid out with rather more formality and their ditches seem to have been recut. Even at what were apparently defended sites those ditches provide evidence of placed deposits, including meat joints and human remains. Inside the enclosures we also find pit deposits containing elaborate artefacts. Houses can still be found on these sites, but the growing evidence for consumption and for the complex treatment of the dead suggests that these earthworks played a more significant part in ritual and ceremonial.

Michelsberg enclosures occupy the pivotal point in the sequence. They are widespread and surprisingly uniform. So many have been found as a result of air photography that a recent issue of the German magazine Archäologie in Deutschland (October–December, 1991) recently made them its principal theme. Many of the enclosures are causewayed and a significant number have more than one ditch (illus 44, 45). The earthworks are often accompanied by palisades, and the causeways are sometimes emphasised by complicated entrance structures. The contents of the ditches resemble the pit deposits of this period and generally include human remains as well as groups of animal bones. They can be found close to the causeways, although these features tend to provide the main target for modern excavation. The sites are later than any of the flat cemeteries, but they extend into the distribution of megalithic tombs, and an enclosure at Caldern which includes a deposit of human bones is located within 100 metres of one of those monuments (Raetzel-Fabian 1991).

Some of the German enclosures are still interpreted as settlements, but apart from the small group of sites that I mentioned earlier, their counterparts in France lack such

44
Crop marks of the
causewayed
enclosure at
Salzkotten-
Oberntudorf,
Germany.
Photograph:
Westfälisches
Museum für
Archäologie, by
courtesy of Dr
Klaus Günther.

associations. The enclosures in the Paris Basin are found in a period which is without either cemeteries or tombs. The main feature of these sites is the virtual ubiquity of deposits of human bone, and these tend to be found in the later levels of the enclosure ditches. Skull fragments are particularly common. We know most about the deposits inside the well-preserved enclosure at Noyen-sur-Seine (Mordant & Mordant 1977). A number of artefact types have concentrated distributions within the excavated part of this site, in particular quernstones which seem to have been deliberately broken before they had seen much use. The same applies to concentrations of pottery and to one group of axe fragments. The animal bones from this area also tend to be found in groups and can be associated with ceramic figures, both of humans and animals. Human bones, including a perforated skull, came from the interior and the ditch. Although there were areas of cobbling inside the earthwork, there was no convincing trace of domestic buildings like those found at other sites of this date, and the only other feature to be identified with any certainty was a row of hearths. Otherwise this area contained a series of tips of cultural material, which seem to have remained undisturbed after they were deposited. Further finds came from the perimeter of the site, and in this case there were placed deposits within the bedding trench for a palisade. Similar deposits were found on other sites in the area, including further figurines and Chasséen vase supports. The latter are a widely distributed ceramic type which is often found in association with mortuary monuments (Burkill 1984, 51–4).

45
Section of one of the excavated ditches at Salzkotten-Oberntudorf, Germany. Photograph: Westfälisches Museum für Archäologie, by courtesy of Dr Klaus Günther.

The enclosures that I have just described extend beyond the limits of Linearband-keramik colonisation. They were apparently created during a period when settlement was more ephemeral but possibly more extensive, and the emphasis on deposits of animal remains may echo their increasing importance in the subsistence economy. The monuments themselves exhibit a greater formality and more emphasis seems to have been placed on the provision of regular openings through the perimeter earthwork. These even extend to a palisaded enclosure at Noyen-sur-Seine which shares this characteristic layout. The separate lengths of ditch certainly provide a focus for formal deposits in a way that does not seem to have happened with Linearbandkeramik earthworks, but it is difficult to say why this very distinctive layout should have been adopted so widely, and over such a long period of time. One possibility is that it was intended to stress the openness of the enclosure to people in the surrounding landscape; another idea is that each length of the perimeter was the concern of a different group. At all events these ideas converge in suggesting that such enclosures served a wider population.

At a quite different level these earthworks represent a complete transformation of the original concept, as we find it in the Linearbandkeramik. The traditional design is maintained and even enhanced, but its significance has been reinterpreted. The first enclosures of this kind were directly associated with settlement sites. They were integrated into the intensive use of nearby areas of the landscape. They might be located directly alongside groups of houses or might even define the limits of particular settlements. Even when they were built on abandoned occupation sites, they may have been located in open spaces within the older settlement where communal activities had always taken place. That was the pattern which we saw at Aldenhoven Site 9. At the same time, some of the settlements so closely bound in with the earliest enclosures were associated with flat cemeteries. These formed a focus for specialised deposits of grave goods, but little evidence of structured deposition has been found in excavation of the enclosures.

The later enclosures, and in particular those associated with Michelsberg and Chasséen pottery, depart from this arrangement in practically every respect. The only exception is the increasingly widespread practice of defining the enclosures by interrupted ditches and palisades. There is less evidence for settlements inside these earthworks, particularly on the sites in northern France, and little sign of occupation in the vicinity. In fact some of the French enclosures adopted upland positions some way beyond the likely limits of settlement (Burkill 1984). The concentration of unusual deposits associated with the edges of these sites may have emphasised the special nature of the perimeter and could even have provided a kind of protection against the world outside. Now the enclosure was the focus for  more specialised activities, which probably included feasting and the deposition of artefacts that may have been employed in rituals. These sites also witnessed animal sacrifice and the rites of passage of the dead. In contrast to the Linearbandkeramik pattern of flat cemeteries, these enclosure could have provided a specialised arena in which human relics were displayed.

◆ ◆ ◆

Finally, we need to consider how far these patterns were changed with the adoption of causewayed enclosures along the Atlantic and North Sea coastlines where there are suggestions of a well-established Mesolithic population. We can consider three areas here: Britain, west central France and southern Scandinavia. The case for a Mesolithic background to these developments is not uniformly strong; it is more convincing in Scandinavia than the other areas, but for the purposes of this presentation all three can be treated together.

Although the chronological sequence varies (causewayed enclosures were adopted first in Britain and only later in the other two regions), developments in all three areas show striking similarities. The source for the enclosures in each of these regions seems to have been amongst the developments that I have just described: the use of earthwork enclosures for specialised rituals in a largely dispersed pattern of settlement. But in each case the enclosures are found in areas with substantial mortuary monuments.

There are strong similarities between the ways in which these enclosures were used during their early phases. In each area they are associated with very similar deposits to those in Germany and northern France: concentrations of animal bones, fine pottery and human remains. In Britain and Scandinavia these are also found in pits inside the monuments. Certain features are strongly represented in all three groups of sites, in particular finds of non-local artefacts, especially axes. For example, on the French site of Machcoul sixty percent of the polished axes came from Plussulien over 150 kilometres away (L'Helgouac'h 1988), and one of the Danish sites may even have been associated with a hoard of copper artefacts originating in Central Europe (Madsen 1988, 309). The British case will be better known. The late levels at a number of the enclosures contained axes produced in distant parts of the country, whilst the causewayed enclosures in Wessex include pottery made in south-west England (Bradley & Edmonds in press).

In each of these areas the segmented layout of the enclosure seems to have been particularly important. At a site like Hambledon Hill, it was carefully maintained when the ditches were recut (Mercer 1988), and at many of the enclosures specific deposits were made against the causeways. These range from the human burials at Champ Durand (Joussaume 1988) to the offerings of meat in the enclosure ditch at Windmill Hill (Smith 1965, 41–2). In Denmark the importance of the segmented ditch was marked in a special way and at Sarup each separate length of earthwork was enclosed by a fence (Andersen 1988: illus 41). This unusual arrangement echoes the gate structures found on sites in the Rhineland but its closest parallel may be at the Trundle in West Sussex (Curwen 1931, pl 1, 107–9).

The deposits found in the segmented ditches of British enclosures are echoed by the finds from features within these monuments, but a similar range of artefacts also seems to have been buried in more isolated pits (Thomas, J 1991, ch 4). Some of the same categories of material extend to the forecourts and flanking ditches of contemporary mortuary mounds. The deposits associated with the Scandinavian enclosures again built upon an existing tradition of offerings, but this time it was associated mainly with bogs and other wet places. Those deposits were most numerous in the early part of the Neolithic period and are found in a series of

regional groups, each of which favours one particular kind of offering: decorated pots containing food, amber beads or stone axes. When the enclosures were created, the frequency of these finds decreased and the same kinds of material were deposited together at the newly built monuments (Bradley 1990, 57–61).

I mentioned that the enclosures in all three areas also include human remains. These are often skulls. In each area it seems likely that the practices taking place at the enclosures were closely linked with those associated with mortuary monuments, but the relationship varies from one area to another. The enclosure at Champ Durand contained a series of burials as well as more fragmentary remains and the excavator suggested that it may have taken over the role of local passage tombs (Joussaume 1988). In Denmark, on the other hand, passage tombs of similar date can be found close to these sites. Some of the enclosures in Britain show the same relationship to long barrows, but in this case the human remains from the enclosures are mainly those of young people who are under-represented at mortuary monuments (Mercer 1988).

These similarities are striking and obviously reflect a common background in the developments that I considered earlier. In all three areas there is little to suggest that the majority of the enclosures were constructed as settlements, and some of those in southern England were located in marginal areas, within woodland clearings (Thomas, K 1982). What is very striking is that both in Britain and on the Continent the enclosures exhibit a rather similar sequence in which certain of the sites assumed a domestic role at a late stage in their history.

The British evidence has come to light only recently and probably concerns only a small number of sites. In certain cases it is clear that enclosures were remodelled. After a long sequence of recutting in which the form of the causewayed ditch was carefully maintained, these features were finally removed, leaving a continuous earthwork. The ramparts could have been reconstructed and were provided with substantial gateways (eg Mercer 1988). Inside these enclosures there is convincing evidence of houses, although it is obvious that these locations were also used in rituals. There is a tendency for the sites that were remodelled to be located in defensible positions, and there is certainly a close relationship between the enclosures that underwent a reconstruction of this kind and those with traces of houses in their interior. In a few instances we find late long barrows, or possibly Neolithic round barrows, very close to the defences. In contrast to the mixture of human bones found beneath most long mounds, these contain one or two articulated burials accompanied by grave goods (Bradley in press). All this evidence seems to suggest that a limited number of specialised enclosures were appropriated as defended settlements at a late stage in their history. They might well have provided the power base of a small section of society. Several of these earthworks are associated with concentrations of arrowheads and even appear to have been attacked and burnt. After that time there is little evidence for the continuous use of these locations, although they may have contributed to later developments, including the adoption of henges and stone circles.

A very similar sequence has been identified in west central France, although it has not been traced in so much detail. Here Joussaume (1988) suggests that the

Neolithic enclosures were built in two distinct phases (cf Joussaume & Pautreau 1990, ch 6, ch 7). As we have seen, in the first phase they had causewayed ditches and were associated with deposits of non-local artefacts and with finds of human remains. Again a number of these sites were remodelled and the causewayed ditches were replaced by continuous earthworks forming a defensive scheme of some complexity. The gateways were the key points in the new design and were protected by massive outworks not unlike those found at British hillforts. The ramparts too were strengthened and were provided with massive stone walls. Unfortunately, we know all too little about the use and history of these sites, but in this case it seems as if they went out of use in the Late Neolithic after a substantial period without any obvious signs of violent destruction. Like the sites in Britain, they provide further evidence for the deposition of human remains in the later parts of the sequence.

Lastly, there is the evidence from southern Scandinavia, and this does exhibit a significant contrast with the other two areas. In this case there is no evidence that the earthworks were converted to defended sites. Instead, it is becoming clear they formed the focus for very large open settlements, which extended across the limits of the original enclosures (Madsen 1988). When that happened it appears that the ditches lost their function. Apart from the multi-period enclosure at Sarup (Andersen 1988), we know very little about their internal features, but they seem to have been larger, and quite possibly richer, than their counterparts on sites which lacked any earthworks. Even so, they present the same basic sequence as those in Britain and western France. The enclosures were created as specialised ritual centres and only assumed a domestic role at a late stage in their history. When that happened, the earthworks lost their importance entirely.

<hr />

◆ ◆ ◆

I have been talking about these monuments as the expression of ideas, and, in particular, about the way in which a single stereotyped design, an enclosure with a causewayed ditch, was reinterpreted and changed from one cultural setting to another. It will be clear by now that there is no one interpretation of these monuments. The reductionist approach which talks about labour organisation fails to account for much of the evidence, and so do attempts to make them all into settlements, cemeteries or, for that matter, anything else. Within the rules that dictated that enclosures should follow this characteristic ground-plan there was enormous scope for local ingenuity. In no sense were the people who built these earthworks imprisoned by convention. In fact their inventiveness is responsible for a complex archaeological sequence.

I have discussed a large number of sites, of different periods and different cultural affiliations, and have considered examples as far apart as Czechoslovakia and Sweden. It would be impossible to summarise this material without repeating much of the detail. What I can do is to emphasise some of the contrasts that we have observed and some of the broader patterns that underlie the changing deployment of causewayed enclosures.

First, there have been variations in their geographical setting. We have seen how their locations changed from a close integration with settlement areas in the

Linearbandkeramik to their construction on the edge of the contemporary landscape in the British Isles. This reflects important changes in the role of these particular monuments, from a vital component of domestic life to a specialised ritual focus.

Secondly, there seem to have been changes in the scale and formality of these earthworks. Most of the earliest sites were small and only a minority were defined by interrupted ditches, yet by the latter part of the sequence the causewayed enclosure was the dominant type and could be built on an enormous scale. This is apparent at a number of widely separated locations, from Urmitz to Hambledon Hill. The growing importance of causeways is matched by the creation of elaborate entrance structures and by the presence of interrupted palisades. Most of these were associated with ditch systems but occasionally they formed enclosures in their own right.

Another striking feature of the sequence is the increasing scale of consumption in evidence at these sites. The oldest enclosures may have been used in some of the activities originally associated with Linearbandkeramik settlements but these may have been fairly informal and certainly were limited in scope. At later enclosures, on the other hand, we find concentrations of specialised artefacts like figurines or vase supports, and groups of non-local types such as axes. There is also evidence for feasting and the sacrifice of animals. It seems entirely probable that more specialised transactions took place at these locations.

We observed a parallel development by which these enclosures became involved in the treatment of the dead. It seems no coincidence that this began after flat cemeteries had gone out of use and that sometimes this happened in regions in which mortuary monuments were absent. Where the two do overlap, the emphasis seems to be on the collective deposition of human remains and on the circulation of unfleshed bone. Most probably the enclosures played some part in the rites of passage, and these could have provided a context for the other activities I have mentioned.

Lastly, the sequence turned full circle and some of the enclosures were transformed into settlement sites. Some became open settlements and others were defended, just like the settlements of the late Linearbandkeramik over a thousand years before. This development is associated with sites on the agricultural margin where megalithic tombs are also found. It shows some similarity to the sequence I described in the first lecture, and here again the creation and operation of monuments may have formed part of the process by which people who had depended on wild resources came to make a commitment to agriculture. If so, the beginning and end of my history of enclosures have another point in common, although no one involved in building these extraordinary monuments would have been able to foresee the unfolding of this complicated sequence. That is our privilege, and we must use it to good effect.

We can only do justice to the people whom we study if we allow them the same inventiveness as we allow ourselves. This interpretation of some Neolithic monuments is simply an idea for discussion. I suggest that the same can be said of the causewayed enclosure itself.

5

THE LOGIC OF MONUMENT BUILDING

The previous lecture showed how monuments and the ideas associated with them could be changed from one area to another. The same process of interpretation can also take place within the local sequence. Using the evidence from Britain and France, this lecture explores the ways in which monuments were adapted and renewed in relation to changing social circumstances. In particular, it focuses on the phenomenon of 'monument complexes' and studies the distinctive manner in which they developed. It consider the recent suggestion that some of these were pilgrimage centres, contending that the use and operation of particular monuments within these complexes was one way in which political relations were played out.

If monuments operate on a different time scale from everyday affairs, they also pose special problems, for they are encountered by successive generations who see them from different perspectives. As archaeologists we are constantly reminded how our own vision is limited, how our view of the ancient world can never be completely free of the concerns of our own time. We can learn from these limitations. Monuments may stay the same when societies change. Like archaeologists today, people in the past would have been forced to engage in acts of interpretation, and that very process can tell us something of their shifting preconceptions.

We considered one aspect of this problem when we followed the history of Neolithic enclosures, but that was a history in which a single kind of monument was interpreted and **re**interpreted from one area to another. No doubt this process of playing off the stereotyped character of those enclosures against the different settings in which they were adopted helped us to identify some of the broader developments in Neolithic Europe, but such an extensive study involved a loss of detail at the local level. I would like to redress this now. Having discussed the way in which monuments embody ideas, we must also consider the process of interpretation that takes place during the history of individual sites.

I have referred to the standing stones of the Kilmartin valley, and in the last lecture I mentioned the Temple Wood stone circle. At different times I have also considered the northern British habit of incorporating fragments of carved rock in the structure of burial cairns. I made these observations in passing, but now it is time to bring them together. Why, for instance, is one of the stones at Temple Wood decorated with two concentric circles (Scott 1989, fig 12), whilst a rather similar stone was found only a short distance away beneath one of the Nether Largie cairns (Craw 1931, fig 6)? Why is the capstone covering the central burial on that

site so profusely decorated? And why is it so important that this stone had been carved more than once?

It rained on my visit to Kilmartin, and the cist slab is under cover Like the dead before me, I sheltered below the cairn, and this was why I spent so long looking at the famous capstone (illus 46). From the start I could agree that the carvings were of more than one phase; as others had observed, the depictions of metal axes are superimposed on an array of cup-marks (Shee 1972, 231, note 5). But how would that make sense if the carving was prepared for a specific funeral? Was the ceremony delayed whilst the stoneworkers changed their minds? Was the cover stone retrieved after an interval in the ground and decorated a second time? There is no evidence of this, and in fact the sequence must have been even longer, for one section of the slab seems to have flaked away after the cup-marks were created, yet the newly exposed surface was decorated in the same style. The edge of this fracture also provides the alignment for some of the later axe carvings. That leaves us with three phases rather than two. There is another problem. Towards one end of the stone the cup-marks seem to run out, yet this is precisely the area in which the rock itself is substantially less weathered. How could this have happened? We can make a direct comparison with some of the standing stones in the vicinity (RCAHMS 1988, 126–43). They had been decorated over their entire surface, but, once erected, the basal section of the upright was protected from the elements. The density of cup-marks tends to be lower here, as if further carvings were added after the

46
The cist below Nether Largie North cairn, Argyll, together with its decorated cover slab. Photograph: Historic Scotland.

stone was raised. Was the Nether Largie capstone originally a decorated menhir?

If so, where would it have stood? Inadequate as it is, the excavation report gives us certain clues. Under the cairn there were two small upright stones, one of them decorated with circles, and at roughly the same distance in from the edge of the cairn there was a pit, interpreted as a grave but without any associated finds, and two large stones lying flat. The entire arrangement was surrounded by a stone bank, open to the south-east (illus 47). This also pre-dated the final construction of the cairn. Might this have been the site of a stone circle, demolished when the burial mound was built? If so, the early enclosure could have been associated with the first stone setting. It even shares its axis with more than one of the sites at Temple Wood. In that case the cist slab at Nether Largie might have belonged to an earlier monument; it could have formed part of the circle itself, or more likely, it was a massive outlier. It may be no accident that a natural slab covered with cup-marks is found just beyond this monument (RCAHMS 1988, 118).

Now I recognise that the argument is tenuous, and that the site is too badly dam-aged for these ideas to be put to the test. Even so, it serves to introduce my main point in this lecture. Monuments exhibit more than a structural sequence; they also epitomise a creative process by which the significance of the past was constantly rethought and reinterpreted. Monuments were adapted and altered to conform with changing circumstances. In this way they provide a subtle index of deeper currents in society.

◆ ◆ ◆

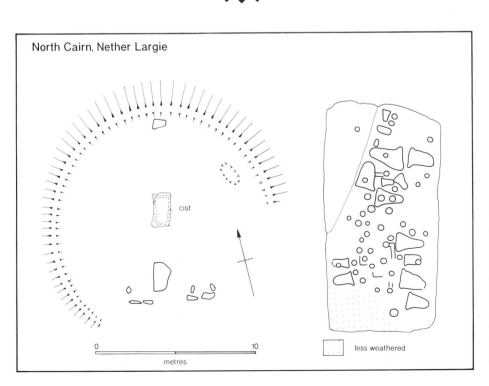

North Cairn, Nether Largie

cist

0   10

metres

less weathered

47
(Left) Outline plan of the excavated features below the North Cairn at Nether Largie (after Craw 1930). (Right) The positions of the carvings on the capstone, showing the line of the early fracture and the part of the stone with less weathering.

But to say that this particular sequence is illustrated at Nether Largie is to rely on a field record of very poor quality. To obtain a clearer illustration of this kind of sequence we must turn to an example from the borderland of history and prehistory. One of the most striking accounts of early Scandinavian society is the description by Adam of Bremen of his visit to the place that we know as Old Uppsala, perhaps the most impressive barrow cemetery in Sweden (Lindqvist 1936; illus 48). As a visitor in the 11th century, he was seeing a great ceremonial centre that had already been established for five hundred years. The mounds constructed at that time covered a series of burials of quite exceptional richness, but the sheer scale of those barrows might well have been influenced by much older constructions in this part of the country, for the surrounding area also contains some of the largest Bronze Age barrows in northern Europe (Jensen 1989, fig 8); the resemblance is so striking that one of these were excavated under the impression that it dated from the Migration Period. Those who created the cemetery at Old Uppsala may have found a source of inspiration in the past, but that is speculation. What is quite clear is that these newly-built mounds formed the focus for considerable activity in later periods, so that the same site was selected for a Viking cemetery. In Adam of Bremen's description the earthworks are no longer the burial places of particular individuals: they are treated as a single phenomenon. There was now a pagan temple on the site, containing images of the gods, and in his account the barrows come together to form a massive amphitheatre from which spectators could watch sacrifices taking place. Close to the temple was a sacred

48
Outline plan of the royal centre at Old Uppsala (after Lindqvist 1936).

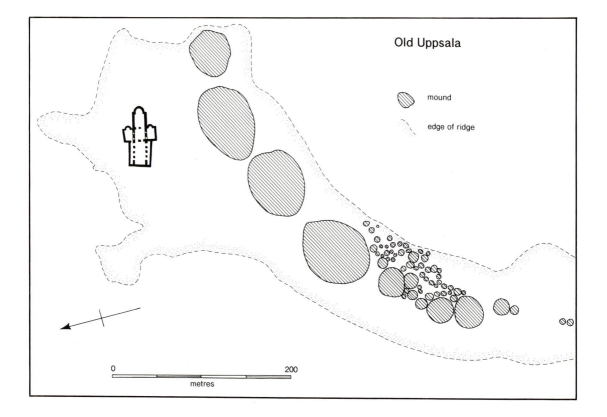

tree. Old Uppsala was now a place of public assembly where the gods were worshipped by the Swedish kings. The sequence of interpretation and reinterpretation continued after Adam's time. By 1164 the pagan gods had been abandoned, but not the site, which was now the see of a Christian bishop.

This sequence involved interpretations of several kinds. The royal graves at Old Uppsala were covered by huge mounds that might well have been modelled on far more ancient prototypes: in a later period this is what happened at Jelling (Hvass 1991, fig 2). Long after their creation, Vikings reinstated its role as a cemetery, and yet by the time of Adam's visit the earthworks were no longer seen as the burial places of particular people: they had coalesced to form the stage setting for rituals involving the gods and the Swedish kings. The focus was no longer on the dead and their position in society; activity centred on a temple, on rituals and on sacrifice. Old Uppsala would change its identity again with the coming of Christianity. These are exactly the nuances that are lost when archaeologists treat each class of monument separately, or fail to appreciate the changing character of the sequence as a whole.

———————— ◆ ◆ ◆ ————————

We can distinguish several different ways in which monuments could develop. Let us begin with Neolithic barrows and cairns. Some monuments never changed their character at all and their history was a short one. At Hazleton North it seems as if a chambered cairn was established, used and then sealed off over a few generations (Saville 1990). Although it occupied a place in the landscape that already had a history of its own, the building of this cairn was an event rather than a process, and it had a finite period of use. In other cases, monuments themselves may not seem to change but the deposits formed in and around them were subject to considerable revision. For example, Bakker's study of Dutch hunebedden suggests that some of them formed the focus for offerings over as many as 400 years (Bakker 1979). Ceramic vessels are especially numerous and appear in a restricted range of forms and decorative motifs. Their use remains unknown, although, as Sherratt suggests, they may have formed stereotyped sets of drinking vessels (Sherratt 1991, 56–7). It is particularly revealing that these deposits usually span several phases, while the finds from contemporary settlement sites cover a much shorter time.

In other cases both the monuments and the deposits within them seem to change. We can consider West Kennet long barrow, like Hazleton North a megalithic tomb belonging to the Severn Cotswold group. In this case there are signs of a complicated structural sequence. The mound was approached through a massive forecourt, yet this was filled in during a later phase in the use of the site. The barrow itself was probably built in stages: first, a quite limited earthwork covering the stone chambers, and, later, a massive 'tail' added to the existing mound. More important, the human remains in the chambers were supplemented by a series of formal deposits extending over a period of perhaps a thousand years (Thomas & Whittle 1986). Similar deposits are found elsewhere in the vicinity. One feature that distinguishes this site from the Hazleton cairn is that newer monuments were established near to West Kennet long barrow. Apart from another long cairn, at Hazleton, they are rare.

96	ALTERING THE EARTH ◆

That forms a link with those cases in which single monuments gradually develop into what we call monument complexes. Again, these come in more than one variety. In some cases they grow by replication, and here we encounter a whole series of constructions of very similar form. A good example is at Passy in eastern France where we find an entire cemetery of long mounds, laid out on two rather similar axes (Thevenot 1985, 199–207; Thevenot *et al* 1988, 58–60). The monument complex is aligned towards some of the areas of contemporary settlement (illus 49), but as so often happens in the Neolithic period, the massive scale of these mounds contrasts sharply with the ephemeral traces of domestic material in their vicinity. The houses of the dead outlasted the dwellings of the living population. This is especially striking in this case as the mounds were built on the site of an older settlement with more substantial domestic buildings.

The alternative is where sites change by diversification, so that monument complexes come into being that bring together a whole variety of different kinds of construction. A good example of this process occurs at Bougon in western France (Rapinot 1986, 458–9; Joussaume & Pautreau 1990, 173–81, 190–5). Here we find five megalithic monuments in the same complex (illus 50). At first sight both the major traditions of mortuary monuments are represented: an Atlantic tradition of building passage tombs with circular cairns, and the more widely distributed tradition of long mounds that we saw at Passy. Recent excavation shows that these monuments were built and rebuilt over more than a thousand years, but the most striking feature of this group is the way in which the forms of different structures were modified and revised. Thus the oldest cairn contains two passage graves, but one of these chambers was converted from a circular to a square ground-plan in order to conform with other developments on the site. At least one similar passage grave, originally contained within a round cairn, was incorporated in the end of a classic long barrow, and it seems quite possible that this mound was actually built to link two passage graves together.

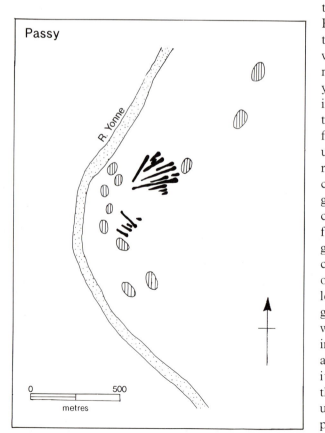

49
Outline plan of the cemetery of long mounds at Passy (black) in relation to areas of contemporary settlement (hatched). (Data from Thevenot *et al* 1988).

Another long mound contains small cists, but it also includes two rectangular passage tombs; again, it may have developed over a considerable period of time. A round cairn with a small stone chamber was apparently enlarged on at least two occasions, once by a rectangular cairn, yet a rather similar monument retained its original form throughout the use of the site although it included two series of burials belonging to quite different periods. The overall sequence is confusing, but its essential character is very easy to grasp. Individual monuments were reinterpreted and rebuilt to conform to changing conventions. They provide an important structural sequence, but they do more than that. They also illustrate how the changing character of the monuments plays on the associations of the site and how new constructions can take over the attributes of their predecessors.

In each case the process of interpretation and reinterpretation is not infinitely varied. Deposits are augmented or changed, the monuments themselves are altered, and new constructions modify our understanding of older ones. In most cases the process is exemplified by a fairly restricted range of architectural sequences. The history of Old Uppsala offers an important lesson here. It is not enough to document the use of monument complexes over long periods of time. In place of 'continuity' there may be evidence of change and reinterpretation. People take what they need from the past, and every reading is selective. Nevertheless, the development of new monuments alongside older examples provides evidence for this process in a particularly explicit manner. The sequence of construction and

50
Outline plan of the megalithic cemetery at Bougon, indicating the possible structural sequence at individual monuments (data from Rapinot 1988 and Joussaume & Pautreau 1990). Note that this diagram summarises the likely phasing at individual monuments and not the sequence on the site as a whole. Sites A, B and E are shown in outline as their pattern of development is not yet clear.

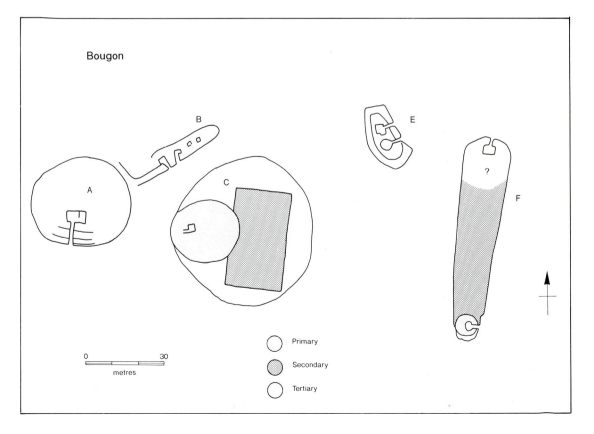

Bougon

0   30
metres

○ Primary

⬤ Secondary

○ Tertiary

modification embodied in a burial ground or a ceremonial centre offers a kind of narrative that is as close as prehistorians can come to writing a political history.

It may be helpful to work from the simple to the complex, and to begin this analysis with those processes affecting single monuments. With that as background, we can then confront the more intractable problems posed by the interpretation of monument complexes. The restricted distribution of such groups means that we must limit the discussion to sites in Britain and France.

◆ ◆ ◆

Not all human constructions are directed at posterity. There are ethnographic instances in which the act of creating something was the only significant feature. When that was complete, the structure had no further importance (eg Küchler 1987). We may find prehistoric monuments which were built and immediately levelled or left to decay. This process is difficult to interpret, but it should not be hard to recognise.

In other cases, we encounter the opposite sequence. This time, the ways in which monuments were constructed facilitated their maintenance over a long period. For example, the creation of earthworks with continuous flat-bottomed ditches, such as those on the major henge monuments, makes them relatively easy to maintain. The cellular construction of some long barrows and long cairns may also permit piecemeal repairs, rather like the hillfort ramparts constructed according to a similar principle (Guilbert 1975). There are other monuments where this could never apply, for example those enclosures defined by interrupted ditches or simply by rings of pits. This form of construction might owe something to the ways in which earthwork building was managed, but there are well-attested cases in which such features appear to have been filled in deliberately. On some sites the monument was never used again, but in other instances these pits were carefully reopened. In this case the very design seems to presuppose a pattern of discontinuous activity, and there are even sites at which the kinds of deposit in the fillings of the original features differ radically from those found in later recuts (eg Barrett *et al* 1991, table 3.12). At the same time, it may not be too much to envisage monuments only parts of which were visible at once. In my third lecture I mentioned the excavators' view that the Maxey cursus represents a project achieved over many generations; at any one time only short lengths of its ditch may have been open (Pryor & French 1985, ch 5). Where earthworks were recut after an interval, the process amounts to more than an episode of repair or maintenance. It may be better to think of it as a re-enactment of the original construction. This is especially true when an elaborate formal plan, such as that of a causewayed enclosure, was recreated after the ditches had filled up completely.

In other cases re-enactment may not be the right term to use and we find evidence of a more radical transformation. Sometimes this happens when the reconstructed monument takes a more durable form than its predecessor. An interesting example of this process is where timber-built monuments were replaced in stone. It would be very easy to see this as evidence of an essential continuity, but there are cases in which environmental evidence suggests an interval of disuse between the decay of the timber uprights and the creation of a later stone setting. This is almost certainly the sequence at Mount Pleasant (Wainwright 1979, ch 2, ch 14), and probably at other sites, and in these cases a number of writers have emphasised how exactly the stone-built monument recreates the layout of a timber setting of which little trace could have remained above ground. These changes could even have been accompanied by a symbolic slighting or stripping of the remains of the older construction. A process of this kind may account for the burning of the timbers and even for a sequence like that at Machrie Moor (illus 51) where there is evidence of some kind of ploughing in between these two phases (Haggarty 1988).

Where the plan of a monument remains substantially unaltered, it is difficult enough to distinguish between repair and re-enactment, but it is still harder to understand sequences in which the monuments also changed their form. There are numerous possibilities, and I shall mention only a few of them here. The original significance of a monument might be enhanced by heightening, extension or expansion, as seems to happen at many individual sites. A few examples serve to illustrate this point. Many of the earthworks that we describe as burial mounds were built up over a considerable period of time, and in cases like Bougon where adequate records exist, it is clear that not every addition to these earthworks coincided with the deposition of burials: some merely affected the scale or appearance of the monument. In the same way, mounds or enclosures could easily be lengthened to create a more striking visual effect. This is perhaps the process that led to the creation of cursuses and bank barrows. But the process involved much more

51
Prehistoric stone
setting on Machrie
Moor, Arran.
Photograph: Historic
Scotland.

than an increase in the size of such monuments, for in certain cases it also brought changes to their form and symbolic significance.

The classic example of this process of enlargement is provided by the Carnac tumuli, for these can be regarded as enormously enhanced versions of the *tertres tumulaires* found in this region of Brittany, those low mounds marked by menhirs that I considered in my second lecture. But in the process of their development the affinities of the Carnac mounds were modified, and tombs of a quite different kind – passage graves – were built against their flanks (Giot *et al* 1979, 218–25). Their relative chronology is disputed, but here we see both the expansion of one kind of monument and the assimilation of another. In like manner, a number of long barrows on the river gravels in England were rebuilt as circular mounds during the Neolithic sequence, so that their basic affinities were altered from a well-established local form of mortuary monument to a tradition of round barrows with quite different symbolic and geographical references (eg Bradley & Chambers 1988). Similar revisions could be effected through the incorporation of relics, in the way that we have already observed in the case of menhirs.

Sometimes the changes that we can recognise on individual sites had other connotations. One particular example is the way in which a number of monuments seem to have been converted from a lunar to a solar alignment during the Neolithic period in Britain. This can be recognised at several levels. There are instances in which the orientation of particular sites was changed as part of the broader sequence of adaptation and reconstruction. This is clearly documented at Stonehenge (Burl 1987, ch 4). The earliest enclosure on this site shares a lunar axis with the nearby long barrows, but the building of the Greater Cursus overlaid this pattern with an alternative alignment on the equinoctial sunrise. Subsequently the entrance to the henge monument was moved to reflect this newer symbolism, and in time the solar axis was given even greater emphasis by the creation of an avenue leading into the surrounding landscape. A rather similar arrangement is evident with the Dorset Cursus which imposed a massive solar alignment on a pattern of existing long barrows which seem to have been directed towards the rising moon (Barrett *et al* 1991, 56).

This last case introduces yet another process in the history of individual monuments, but one which is found very widely. This is where monuments of quite different types and associations are superimposed on one another, as if to subvert the existing meaning of a particular construction. As with the change from timber to stone circles, this development could be emphasised by destroying the older monument, or even by ploughing the site before rebuilding commenced. The pattern is most obvious in those cases where the successive monuments show no resemblance to one another at all. For example, the Maiden Castle bank barrow cuts straight across an existing causewayed enclosure (Sharples 1991, 255–6), whilst the enclosures at Fornham All Saints stand in the same relationship to a cursus monument (Hedges & Buckley 1981, 8). A henge at Thornborough was built on top of another cursus (*ibid*, 31–2) and forms part of a line of circular monuments

which cut across its axis at ninety degrees. There can be a comparable relationship between enclosures and mounds. At Bryn Celli Ddu it seems as if a small passage tomb was superimposed on a ditched enclosure containing a setting of stones (Lynch 1991, 91–101, 339). Rather the same sequence is found at Callanish (P Ashmore pers comm; illus 52), whereas at Newgrange a massive timber circle was built after the collapse of the passage tomb (Sweetman 1985).

Some monuments reveal several changes of this kind. Consider the evidence from Maxey in Cambridgeshire (Pryor & French 1985, ch 2). Here we find an unusual juxtaposition of monuments of different types: an oval barrow, a cursus, two pit circles, a henge and an outsize round barrow, perhaps of Late Neolithic date. Their precise sequence is a matter for discussion but the broad outlines are clear (illus 53). The cursus is probably later than a nearby causewayed enclosure and it obviously pre-dates one of the pit circles, as well as the massive henge. The other chronological relationships are more tenuous, and my interpretation is not the only possibility.

The cursus may have been intended to include the position of the oval barrow, but it is just as likely that this barrow was erected later, within the path of the cursus itself. At all events two pit circles were created nearby, each of them offset from the long axis of the barrow, and one of them cutting across the earthwork of the cursus. Whilst the long barrow still survived, it was incorporated into the entrance of a henge, and at the centre of that new enclosure a massive round barrow was built. This was not perfectly circular and took its long axis from the oval mound. The ditch of the henge was filled in, whilst the same sequence took place during the first structural phase of the round barrow, a circular enclosure with an internal

52
Part of the stone circle at Callanish, Lewis, with the remains of a small passage tomb in the foreground. Photograph: Historic Scotland.

bank and a central mound built of turf. That mound was subsequently enlarged into a massive round barrow filling the entire area inside the older ring ditch.

It is not certain that the henge and the barrow were constructed simultaneously, but the final phase of this mound almost certainly post-dates the levelling of the henge. The juxtaposition of so many monuments cannot be coincidental, since alignments between different earthworks seem to have been important, but the sheer variety of different constructions at this one location suggests that the precise significance of this place underwent radical revision. In the development from causewayed enclosure to cursus, and from cursus to henge, we may claim that we have the orthodox sequence for eastern England, but that misses the point. Most of these monuments were built at exactly the same location and in such a way that each clearly took into account the existence of its predecessor. Rather than thinking of this simply as a stratigraphic sequence, we might consider it as evidence for the ways in which the significance of a single place was reinterpreted over hundreds of years.

So far I have traced the changing history of a number of monuments and the ways in which their meanings may have been modified in successive stages of their history.

53
The likely sequence of monuments on the site of the Maxey henge. (Data from Pryor & French 1985).

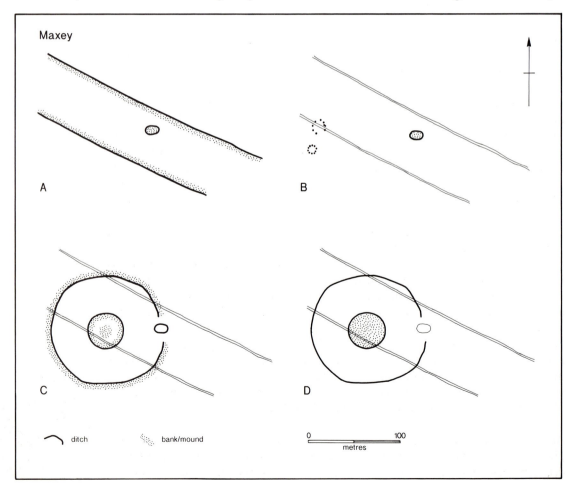

The process extends from subtle modifications by accretion to their destruction and replacement. But in one sense this evidence is atypical, for the argument rests on the evidence of individual sites when such changes are more often found extending across a wider landscape. How were changes effected on this larger geographical scale?

◆ ◆ ◆

In most areas it seems likely that we can identify one primary 'founder' monument, although that is not to deny that these locations may have achieved their significance at a still earlier date. Founder monuments may undergo a process of change and modification along the lines that I have indicated, but it is just as common for them to provide the focus for a series of offerings without any rebuilding at all. For example, one of the cursus monuments mentioned earlier – the Dorset Cursus – clearly provided the focus for a whole series of earthworks and formal deposits despite the fact that its own earthwork was never modified or maintained. It simply established an axis around which later activity was structured (Barrett *et al* 1991, ch 2-4). That accounts for the paradoxical situation that so much Late Neolithic activity focuses on earthworks whose sequence of building and rebuilding ended centuries before (Pryor in press).

Often the founder monument becomes the central point in a wider distribution of sites. But in other cases their spatial relationship can be rather more distinctive. Newer monuments may be aligned directly on existing structures in the landscape, or in appropriate cases they may echo the alignment of the founder monument itself. Alternatively the first monument in such a complex may be drawn into a quite new setting. Sometimes this happens through the process of structural modification that I have described already, but in other cases there may be more direct signs of incorporation. This happens, for example, where a later monument takes in constructions already present in the landscape. Examples might include the incorporation of Breton long mounds in the course of the Carnac alignments or the similar treatment of barrows and small enclosures by cursuses in the British Isles.

One striking feature of these developments is the way in which monuments seem to multiply. A single founder monument appears to spawn a burgeoning variety of other monuments around it, so, for example, a single cursus may provide the focus for a whole series of barrows or hengiform enclosures. Often these sites are only slightly different from one another, yet, once established, they too experience a complex sequence of refurbishment and modification. Indeed, it is perfectly possible that the process I am describing within monument complexes as a whole also takes place on a smaller scale in relation to their individual components. The effect is of a series of Chinese boxes. Thus the Stonehenge area contains a number of henge monuments, most of them built in relation to the distribution of older earthworks, yet inside the largest of these sites – at Durrington Walls – we find evidence of a number of similar constructions (RCHME 1979, 15–18).

At the same time, we can be misled by the most visible components of these complexes into forgetting that among the integral features of these places are formal deposits of cultural material. These are found not only within the features of specific monuments, but also in pits across the supposedly empty areas in between them. For example, both Durrington Walls and Woodhenge certainly contain a wide array of deposits of cultural material, but some of the most unusual finds come from the surrounding area. Indeed, at one site it is known that the positions of pit deposits of this kind had been marked by cairns (Stone 1935). In this sense even pits may once have constituted small-scale monuments. The same is suggested by a recently published excavation at Lawford in Essex, where an unusual deposit of pottery and other artefacts seems to have been enclosed by a ditch (Shennan *et al* 1985).

Another striking concentration of henges is found in the Milfield Basin of north Northumberland (Harding 1981; Miket 1985). Here a number of small enclosures are ranged in a line across the lower ground, but appear to be directed towards both cultural and natural features in the surrounding area. Those cultural features include post settings and standing stones, whilst some of the henge monuments are aligned on distant mountaintops. In contrast to some of my earlier examples, there is no evidence that these sites made use of astronomical observations. At the same time, this complex provides so far unparalleled evidence for the subdivision of the areas in between these henges. A number of pit alignments have been discovered, and it seems likely that these are the remains of internal boundaries within the monument complex (Miket 1981).

◆ ◆ ◆

At this point it may be useful to turn our attention to some more sustained archaeological examples. I should make it clear that what follows is my own interpretation of the archaeological sequence of two sites in the Thames valley which are only six kilometres apart: the cemetery at Barrow Hills, Radley and the cursus complex at Dorchester on Thames. Radley is only published in interim form at present (Lambrick 1990, 10–13), whilst my reading of the structural sequence at Dorchester differs in minor ways from the definitive publication of the site, soon to appear (Atkinson *et al* 1951; Bradley & Chambers 1988). Fortunately, in both cases the character of the overall sequence is not in any dispute.

In some respects the two sequences complement one another; most of the monuments at Dorchester on Thames are Neolithic; many of those at Radley are Bronze Age. We begin with Dorchester on Thames (illus 54). Here it is no longer possible to identify a single founder monument; there seem to be several candidates, and more than one earthwork may have been present from the outset. The earliest features that we can trace appear to be two elongated enclosures, each associated with fragmentary human remains. Both share the same alignment and could have been directed towards the rising moon. The smaller enclosure may also have been aligned on two small mounds, one at either end, although this is not known for certain. One was a round barrow and the other has more in common with the last long barrows.

The first major modification happened when the Dorchester on Thames cursus was built. As we saw on other sites, this adopted a solar alignment, and the eastern section of the monument appears to have been directed towards the midwinter sunrise.

Its surviving terminal incorporated one of the existing enclosures, whilst the course of the monument cut through the long axis of the other one, changing the orientation of the complex as a whole. It also abutted one of the existing mounds, and after the cursus had been built, that earthwork was recreated, changing its outward form from an oval barrow to a round mound (cf Thomas, J 1991, 158–62).

Once that alignment had been established, it influenced the orientation of newer monuments in this complex. A series of small enclosures were built in and around the cursus, all of which were aligned along its main axis. These enclosures took several forms: they could be defined by continuous ditches, by rings of pits, or by a circle of posts, but all came to form the focus for a similar series of deposits in their upper levels. These included human cremations, burnt animal bones and a small selection of elaborate artefacts. On at least one site an existing monument was modified so as to conform to the new scheme, and a ring of pits or possibly post sockets was cut into the structure of an older round barrow; this enclosure had a single entrance facing into the cursus. The finds from the monument also included

54
The likely sequence of development in the monument complex at Dorchester on Thames (after Bradley & Chambers 1988).

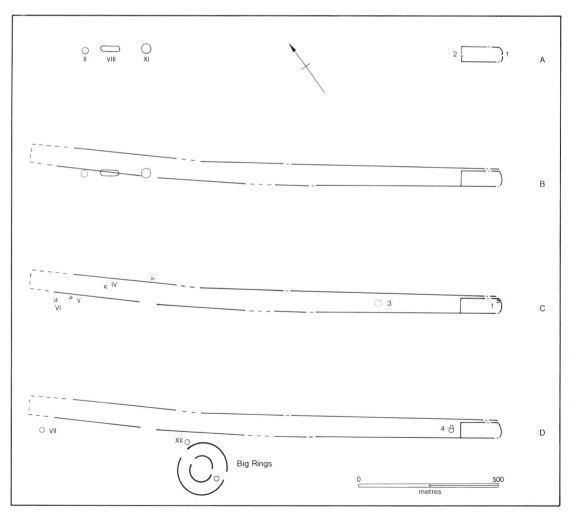

cremated human bone. Although little detail is available, it seems likely that similar deposits were placed in pits in between the monuments.

A common feature of the small enclosures established in and around the cursus was their characteristic sequence of filling and recutting, generally taking place within individual pits; I have discussed similar practices already. This contrasts with the next stage in the sequence when a large henge monument, much like that at Thornborough, was established next to the cursus. Its relationship to earlier monuments is revealing. In contrast to the hengiform enclosures, this had a massive flat-bottomed ditch which could be maintained over a lengthy period, and in this case there is no sign of the characteristic sequence of filling and recutting. In contrast to the other monuments, it contained deposits of Beaker pottery. Its alignment was quite different from the axis established by the cursus, but like the henge monument at Maxey, this site incorporated an existing barrow or circular enclosure in its entrance.

That henge monument then assumed a role as the focus for a barrow cemetery of Beaker and Early Bronze Age date. One mound was built against its entrance and another in the centre of the Neolithic cursus. The remaining barrows extended right across the surrounding area. There is even evidence for the deposition of a human cremation on the site of a nearby post circle several hundred years after the building itself had been destroyed by fire.

This sequence illustrates some of the points that I made earlier. There is a striking difference between the cursus, the large henge and virtually all the other monuments on the site. The largest monuments were clearly built to last and their earthworks were constructed in such a way that they could easily be maintained. This did not apply to most of the smaller enclosures, where the archaeological sequence involved episodes of construction, reconstruction and the careful deposition of cultural material. Secondly, the changes of alignment illustrated by this complex have a much wider resonance. The first monuments seem to have adopted a lunar alignment, but this was entirely changed by the imposition of the cursus which dictated a new axis for the complex as a whole. Similarly, that alignment was finally abandoned when the large henge monument was built. Again, the construction of a major earthwork corresponds with wider changes in the character of this site, and in particular, its development as a barrow cemetery. Lastly, the entire sequence involves a subtle interplay between new developments and modifications to the forms of existing monuments. Thus the change from a solar to a lunar alignment also required the reorientation of older earthworks, which were brought together as component parts of a new design. In just the same way, when the main henge monument was built, its entrance seems to have incorporated a mound or enclosure located alongside the cursus: we saw exactly the same relationship at Maxey. In other cases the same changes were achieved by modifying the form of existing features. That may be why an oval barrow was reconstructed as a round mound, belonging to a quite different tradition of earthwork building, and why in a later phase at least one of the mounds was replaced by a pit or post circle related to the structure of the small henges found on the site. At one level we can talk of modification; at another, of reinterpretation.

It was as this distinctive sequence came towards its end that the major period of activity began at Barrow Hills, and in this case we encounter a strikingly different pattern. Again a number of monuments were established following a single alignment, but at this site the focal point was a causewayed enclosure (illus 55). This had been accompanied by another late long barrow, as well as a series of mortuary deposits, but the earthwork had experienced no structural changes for several centuries, and Late Neolithic artefacts are rare in its secondary levels.

The later monuments at Barrow Hills also follow a single alignment, but in this case it consists of two rows of circular mounds and other features directed towards the position of the older enclosure. The first of these were probably built towards the end of the Neolithic period, whilst the others, mainly conventional round barrows, span the Beaker ceramic phase and the full extent of the Early Bronze Age. Many of the mounds underwent substantial modification during their history, accompanied by a wide variety of mortuary deposits. In fact some of the graves contained an unusually varied range of artefacts. In a few cases monuments of different kinds may have replaced one another directly, most obviously a pond barrow which was superimposed on the remains of a Neolithic ring ditch. In turn the outer ditch of a round barrow cut through the filling of this feature.

These prominent monuments were supplemented by specialised deposits. Late Neolithic pits were found near to the early ring ditches and again they seem to have been filled with a certain formality. The basic axis of the cemetery was also echoed by a row of urned cremations. There were a significant number of other deposits of human bone within the apparently empty spaces in between the mounds. The orientation of the cemetery never changed, yet by the time that this complex achieved its fullest extent, the causewayed enclosure had remained unaltered for more than a thousand years.

In this case there is less evidence of change than we saw at Dorchester on Thames. The cemetery retained a single axis throughout its history, and the role of the

55
Outline plan of the cemetery at Barrow Hills in relation to the Abingdon causewayed enclosure. (Data from Lambrick 1990 and Bradley in press).

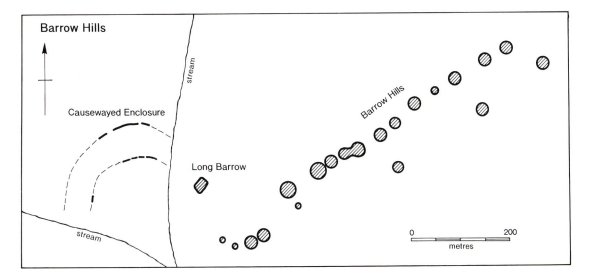

causewayed enclosure as the founder monument never seems to have been challenged. Despite its considerable antiquity, it remained the focus of the barrow cemetery from the Late Neolithic period until the end of the Early Bronze Age. In this case we can supplement the evidence from the excavated monuments by a wide variety of deposits found in the surrounding area. By no means all of these contained human remains, but they still served to emphasise the alignment followed by the monuments of the cemetery.

We have now considered the development of individual monuments and the growth of two representative monument complexes. It is when we combine the two that certain broader trends become apparent, and, I suggest, it is these that have most to tell us about the logic of monument building.

Again it will be helpful if we focus on a few well-documented contrasts. First of all, it is worth distinguishing between the multiplication of virtually identical monuments in the same complex and the presence of a greater variety of constructions. Thus the Milfield Basin contains a strikingly uniform range of small henge monuments, spaced across a considerable area of land (Harding 1981; Miket 1985). Those differences that are apparent between them can only be recognised as a result of excavation, and, as we shall see, they owe less to contrasts that were evident from the start than they do to divergent sequences of development. At the other extreme are monument complexes like those known close to Avebury or Mount Pleasant, where the effect of recent fieldwork has been to increase the sheer variety of information that is available. Such areas include the conventional range of long barrows, causewayed enclosures and henges, but they also contain monuments that are very far from standard. There is the enormous pit circle of Maumbury Rings and the palisaded enclosure under the modern town of Dorchester (Bradley 1975; Woodward et al 1984); and at Avebury there is Silbury Hill and the array of palisaded enclosures found nearby (Whittle 1991).

Secondly, the similarities that are apparent between monuments in the same complexes should not blind us to the fact that these sites can be associated with material culture or depositional practices of strikingly different types. For example, in the Milfield Basin three monuments apparently of similar form and date have radically different artefact associations: Beaker pottery in one case, and in the other instances two variant forms of Grooved Ware. In south Dorset, large amounts of Grooved Ware and its associated artefacts have been found in the perimeter of Mount Pleasant (Wainwright 1979), but the palisaded enclosure at Greyhound Yard contains very little material (Woodward et al 1984). Maumbury Rings, on the other hand, was quite prolific (Bradley 1975), but the deposits on this site have little in common with the practices evidenced at Mount Pleasant and are much more like those in the pit circle henge at Wyke Down thirty kilometres away (Barrett et al 1991, 92–106).

There is a still more important distinction to be made in the developmental sequence at different monuments. In some cases, for example in the Milfield

Basin, the original henges were strikingly uniform and what differences can be recognised arise from contrasting sequences of development on individual sites. Thus some of these sites remained as simple enclosures, whilst others contained settings of timbers and possibly of upright stones. In some cases the original enclosure was also contained inside a wider setting of uprights, whilst the central area of the site could eventually be used for burial. Very much the same sequence could be present at stone circles in northern Britain. In fact, a particularly striking example is provided by Temple Wood.

On the other hand, the monuments in the Milfield Basin remain small scale. They exhibit a very limited range of sizes, and in this sense they constitute what John Barnatt calls an 'equal component' monument complex (1989, 153). This is by no means universal, and almost as often we find evidence that one particular monument has been built on a far larger scale than all the others. This might be a henge monument like Avebury, a mound like Silbury Hill or an immense passage grave like that at Knowth, but the contrast is very evident. For example, we need to ask ourselves why south Dorset contains such a remarkable range of Late Neolithic enclosures, entirely dominated by a few sites built on a larger scale than their counterparts in the same area. By contrast at Knowlton, only thirty kilometres away, the range of structures appears to be more limited (RCHME 1975, 113–15). Three of the henges are of the same order of magnitude, whilst only the Great Circle has been built on a larger scale.

The comparison becomes even more revealing when we recognise two other features of these groups. There seems to be evidence for a process by which each complex is dominated by only one outsize monument of any single kind; this is essentially a much more massive version of the features found elsewhere in the same complex. Thus Maumbury Rings is a massive version of the simple pit circles found nearby on Conygar Hill (Woodward & Smith 1987, 84–6; illus 56), whilst Mount Pleasant illustrates the same process as it affects timber circles. I also mentioned the cemetery at Knowth. Here the stratigraphic sequence is particularly revealing (Eogan 1986, ch 2, ch 3). A ring of small passage tombs of uniform size were built facing into what seems to have been an empty area. That space was later appropriated by a gigantic circular mound, which clearly overlay two of the existing constructions. It is as if certain complexes are distinguished by containing one enormous example of a particular kind of monument. In most areas its construction seems to close off further development.

It may be no accident that complexes with one dominant monument of this kind often occur in a similar setting. One effect of systematic field survey has been to show that some of the largest monuments were located in areas with quite a low density of surface finds. Much the same amount of material occurs elsewhere in the surrounding region. But if these monument complexes do not seem to have been at the heart of the settlement pattern, they certainly occupied locations that were readily accessible; for example, the small groups of monuments in the Upper Thames valley are nearly always located at the confluence of the river and its tributaries (Thomas, J 1991, figs 7.3, 7.4). On a national level it has been suggested that important monuments were built in such places in order to command the major

routes by which exotic artefacts were distributed. I would propose an amendment to this argument. In general terms it is the largest monument complexes, and those with the widest range of structures, that seem to form the focus for concentrations of non-local objects. These sites may also include a range of structural elements that are unusual or absent in the surrounding area. In each case we can make rather similar observations: these complexes were located for ready accessibility; they could have drawn on a particularly large catchment; and they contain an abnormally wide range of references to distant places and practices, both through the character of the associated artefacts and through the occasional echo of exotic building traditions. All these elements tend to be found together, so that the Avebury complex, for example, includes an usually wide range of non-local axes but also contains an outsize mound whose likely prototypes may be in Ireland or northern England. In the same way, the enormous monuments around Carnac are closely linked with a concentration of imported artefacts or raw materials. At one level we can recognise a contrast between monument complexes like those in Northumberland, which seem

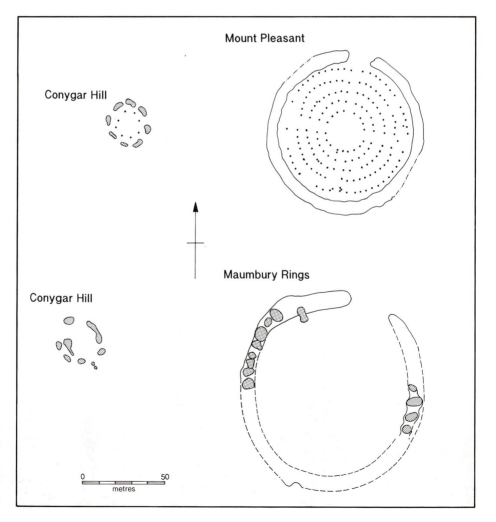

56
The range of sizes shown by monuments of the same kind at Dorchester, Dorset. (After Bradley 1975, Wainwright 1979 and Woodward & Smith 1987).

to emphasise the importance of place, and others where the form and associations of these sites suggest a greater emphasis on networks. In this case the range of monument types is echoed by the range of exotic references.

In his study of Neolithic Orkney, Colin Renfrew accounts for this paradoxical situation by suggesting that social networks were established through the use of certain places for pilgrimage (1985, 255–6). There may be something in the idea. But that interpretation would account for only some of these observations. He is surely right to identify the the importance of non-local elements, but in itself his argument is not sufficient to explain the distinctive way in which these complexes developed through time.

◆ ◆ ◆

I began with an analogy from the historical period. I would like to end by comparing the development of monument complexes with some evidence from the Classical world. The so-called inter-polity sanctuaries such as Delphi and Olympia have certain characteristics in common with these monument complexes (illus 57). Again the major constructions never appear in isolation. These sites contain a whole series of temples and treasuries operated by different *poleis* (Morgan 1990). The sanctuaries are outside the ambit of normal settlement and form a focus not only for dealings with the gods but also for highly formalised competition between the constituent groups. This is most evident from the famous institution of the games, but it is also illustrated by the practice of erecting conspicuous statues to the victors, statues which could be identified with the polities from which they came (Raschke 1988). There may be further evidence of competitive emulation in other media. The provision of votive offerings is a major feature of the sanctuary sites and the emphasis on the deposition of arms and armour suggests that this process could amount to a kind of surrogate conflict. Moreover, Anthony Snodgrass (1986) has argued that the building of temples and treasuries was yet another example of a process of political competition played out through ritual and ceremonial. Temples or treasuries in widely separated areas were built to copy, and

57
A 19th century reconstruction of the sanctuary at Olympia. (From Gardner 1925.)

even to trump, one another's distinctive architecture. Nearly all these interpret-ations are controversial, but it is certainly true that these kinds of display and com-petition are found away from the core areas of the contending parties and at a time when Greek society was undergoing a dramatic change.

Of course it would quite wrong to suppose that the Greek sanctuaries provide a close analogy for the monument complexes that we find in Britain and north-west France. What they do provide is a graphic example of two much wider principles: the subdivision of the ritual arena between different groups who were not ordinarily resident in the area; and a process by which strains between those communities might be played out through the media of ritual and monument building. It is at this level that our discussion is best conducted.

I have argued that a process of interpretation and reinterpretation was fundamental to the development of prehistoric monuments and monument complexes. It accounts for a whole series of distinctive patterns in the way in which these sites developed over time, but the grouping of superficially similar constructions in the same location has always posed special problems, and these are not addressed by treating the complex as a whole as some kind of 'central place'. This does not take into account enough of the available evidence (cf Bonnanno *et al* 1990). Monuments that were very similar in form in fact developed side by side, accomp-anied by deposits containing non-local artefacts or items of material culture that referred to connections with distant areas. Some of the monuments also incorpor-ated structural devices that were best matched in remote parts of the country, as if to reinforce the message provided by the consumption of exotica. There seems to be a relationship between the sheer scale of different monument complexes and their siting at particularly accessible positions in the landscape, as if labour might have been contributed by people coming from a considerable area. Most important of all, certain of these sites witness the growth of one dominant monument at the expense of all the others, as if contests over the right interpretation of the world were to be settled by the sheer scale of the construction project.

All these elements appear to be related to one another, and they form the culmin-ation of a process of interpretation and reinterpretation that in some areas had been going on for hundreds of years. However different the emphases shown by local developments, the end of the sequence often looks the same, for the construc-tion of one enormous monument served both to fix what had previously been a partial view of the world and to bring this entire process to an end. It is followed by the adoption of new practices and a new material culture, both of which demon-strate even more explicitly the role of powerful groups. It may be no coincidence that the areas which saw the most energetic competition in the construction and operation of monuments also saw the precocious adoption of new forms of display in life and death. The sequences treated in such detail in the closing section of this lecture entered a new phase with the adoption of Beaker pottery and metalwork. It is my contention that this should not be seen as the advent of a new system, sweep-ing away the traditions that had served the population for a millennium. For the parties involved it was nothing less than the logical culmination of that process.

6

EPILOGUE

THE AFTERLIFE OF MONUMENTS

By their very nature monuments survive over long periods of time. The process of interpretation described in the previous lecture did not end during the prehistoric period: it still concerns us today. The final lecture considers how certain monuments were reinterpreted in the early Medieval period when particular examples, ranging in date from Neolithic to Roman times, were brought back into use as high status sites. This process can be compared with the invention of traditions and in certain cases served to legitimise the position of new elites. Even the selection of sites for renewal shows a certain patterning, and this may shed light on the origin myths of different groups in the post-Roman world. The argument is illustrated by 'royal sites' in the British Isles.

I return one last time to my starting point in Mid Argyll. There is an extraordinary range of monuments in this area, but if there is one site which dominates all the others, I have said little about it so far. This is Dunadd, that distinctive lump of rock set between the uplands and the sea (RCAHMS 1988, 149–59; illus 58). It owes its wider fame to its pivotal role in the post-Roman world, when it was one of the high status fortifications of Dalriada. Like sites of similar eminence elsewhere, its position may have been determined partly by its natural appearance. It is essentially a place turned into a monument, but I wonder whether that is the whole story.

Consider its setting in Argyll. It commands a route leading across a narrow tract of land between west Scotland and the Irish Sea, a route important enough to be recreated by the Crinan Canal in the 18th century. It is at the edge of an unusually productive region of low-lying ground, the very area which had attracted such a high density of monuments from the Neolithic period onwards. Yet that last statement carries echoes of the setting of other post-Roman centres. How common it is for these to be found amidst an array of older monuments, yet how rarely is this observation discussed by prehistorians. Once again the archaeology of this small area provokes a train of thought which I would like to develop further.

There is a case to be made that Dunadd had a prehistory to match its eminence in the historic period, but that case, I accept, is a weak one. There are Neolithic and Bronze Age artefacts from the site, one of them (a Neolithic stone ball) of a specialised type well outside its usual distribution (RCAHMS 1988, 7). There are standing stones at the foot of Dunadd and there are rock carvings, apparently of prehistoric date, on the outcrop itself (*ibid*, 154). Even the famous inauguration stone – a deep footprint carved into the living rock – is matched by a much fainter petroglyph of the same kind (*ibid*, 157–9). Most probably both date from the post-

Roman period, but similar carvings are known from prehistory, and the difference of preservation could be due to a difference of age. But far more important is the sheer concentration of major monuments in the surrounding area. The distribution of fortified sites visible from Dunadd is not so very different from the distributions of ceremonial enclosures, mortuary cairns and rock art, most of which could still have been identified in the first millennium AD.

That argument for some kind of continuity is tenuous and to some extent unnecessary, but it is an argument that has been championed on the basis of far more detailed studies at other sites of this period. Consider the evidence from the Northumbrian site of Yeavering (Hope-Taylor 1977). At a general level the two areas have much in common. Yeavering is at the edge of the Milfield Basin, another unusually fertile tract of lowland in an essentially upland region, and, like the area around Dunadd, it contains a remarkable array of prehistoric monuments: henges, barrows, rock carvings and hillforts (illus 59). But in this case the excavator of the site explains its location in terms of its history rather than the resources at its command. Again there is a standing stone close to the palace site, and at Yeavering the buildings of the post-Roman complex were located in between two Neolithic or Bronze Age monuments: a round barrow at one end of the site and a stone circle at the other. A henge monument has been identified on the edge of this complex (Harding 1981), and the excavation of the post-Roman buildings produced evidence of a cremation cemetery of Early Bronze Age origin (Hope-Taylor 1977; Ferrell 1990). There were Roman burials in field ditches underneath the palace, and towering over the site, on Yeavering Bell, is one of the largest hillforts in northern England.

58
Dunadd, Argyll: a royal centre of the early historical period. Photograph: Historic Scotland.

At a general level the relationships seem similar, but their interpretation was decisively different. For the excavator of Yeavering the evidence points to an enormously long continuity of public use for ritual and ceremonial, a sequence beginning in the Neolithic period and lasting, perhaps without interruption, through to the first millennium AD (Hope-Taylor 1977). Now I do not find this idea convincing. The prehistoric components of the sequence have been misunderstood and are punctuated by long intervals in which there are no signs of activity on the site. In the same way, the relationship between the prehistoric and the early medieval constructions suggest that the original layout of this complex could no longer be comprehended when the royal centre of Gefrin was built. It is not my intention to go through these detailed objections here, for they are available in print (Bradley 1987b), but to reflect on the character of this kind of sequence and its implications for the afterlife of monuments.

In the last two lectures I talked about a process by which ceremonial monuments developed. In a sense these constructions were adapted to changing circumstances, but in a most individual manner. As we found with public ritual, those changes were only rarely expressed as rupture and outright rejection; more commonly they were achieved by a process of interpretation. The past provided a source of authority no matter how far practices had changed. We saw this in the development of one particular category of monument – the Neolithic enclosure – and also

59
View of the Milfield Basin, Northumberland looking towards the royal site at Yeavering.

in the changing configuration of monuments that make up the ceremonial centres of the British Isles. But in every case the process did have an element of continuity, even if the links with the past were reinterpreted to suit contemporary ideas. That is only one kind of sequence. Monuments could, and did, go out of use. Few of those established in the Neolithic period retained their significance in the different cultural climate of the first millennium BC, and some were even ploughed out (Bradley 1981). It is precisely this hiatus, during the later prehistoric period, that breaches the continuity of ritual observance claimed by the excavator of Yeavering. Once such a hiatus had been allowed to happen, a different kind of history emerged.

It is archaeologists and historians who think in terms of linear time. Archaeologists have field methods for analysing sequence, and specialised procedures for providing dates. Historians work with written sources, scrutinising these for bias and outright error, and comparing different accounts of the same events (cf Goody 1977). But without those skills, or the kinds of raw material to which they are applied, the past loses its orderly appearance. As we know from the work of early antiquarians, enigmatic monuments were attached rather uncritically to the few names known from written sources: to Romans, to Druids, to the Anglo-Saxons. The evidence of place names reveals a similar process. To take a simple example, among the hill-forts of Wessex are sites attributed to Caesar, Vespasian, Hengist, King Alfred, the Welsh and the Danes. If the past is a foreign country, it is a country waiting to be colonised.

As historians have shown so clearly, traditions can be invented (Hobsbawm 1983), or at least they can assume the status of a myth (Cohen 1985, 99). New developments are more secure where they are invested with the authority of the past. That is why origin myths are so important and yet so malleable. It is also why genealogies have to be created. The point is made very clearly in Michael Hunter's discussion of the Anglo-Saxon sense of the past. Describing these genealogies, he says:

> 'Their uniform length and their random combinations of noble-sounding names suggest artificiality, and they were clearly important to contemporaries less for their historical accuracy than for the impression of age they conveyed' (1974, 33).

They would be easy to memorise, for they could be codified in verse with a strict alliterative structure that made them ideally suited for public performance (Sisam 1990). They might contain the names of pagan gods, heroes or characters from Germanic mythology, along with figures from the Roman world. Thus the genealogy of the East Anglian kings includes Julius Caesar but identifies him as the son of Woden. With the coming of Christianity, descent was traced back to Adam, and this is found from Ireland to Scandinavia where the royal line took in Saturn, Jupiter and Priam along the way.

The manipulation of time is central to the argument, but it is not found universally. The reuse of prehistoric monuments may be explained in several ways, and I would be the last to suggest that social explanations need be uppermost. Certain

geographical positions, of which Dunadd is a likely example, are of strategic importance, whilst others control particular resources: agricultural land, trade routes or
mineral wealth. Some monuments might be rebuilt simply because this involved less
work than a new construction; thus the Romans converted a Neolithic henge monument into an amphitheatre (Bradley 1975) and the process was repeated during
later phases when several amphitheatres were reused as fortifications (*ibid*; Thomas,
C 1964; Fulford 1989). It is only where monuments of particular social eminence
are juxtaposed that more detailed discussion is warranted. Even here, the existence
of an overall pattern is more important than any single element.

◆ ◆ ◆

I can illustrate this point with two examples. First, let us return to the evidence
from north Northumberland, where, Bede tells us, successive royal centres were
created at Yeavering and at Milfield. Both sites have been located by air photography and one has been excavated on a large scale (Hope-Taylor 1977;
Tinniswood & Harding 1991). As we saw in my discussion of monument
complexes, the prehistoric earthworks of this area have also been investigated
systematically (Harding 1981). What is so striking is how persistently Neolithic
and Bronze Age sites seem to have been invested with a new significance during
the post-Roman period.

I discussed the Neolithic monuments of the Milfield Basin in the previous lecture.
Although their detailed histories may vary, their basic configuration seems clear.
For the most part the henge monuments are found in a line extending along the
basin, with important outliers to the east and west. Some of these sites were recreated as stone circles, whilst others were accompanied by freestanding posts or
menhirs. In certain cases these uprights enhanced the axis of particular sites, which
tends to be directed towards natural features of the skyline and not at astronomical
events. A few of the henge monuments saw the addition of single burials towards
the end of their history, and Bronze Age round barrows and flat graves are often
found nearby (*ibid*).

60
Outline plans of
the prehistoric
and early
medieval features
at Yeavering.
(Data from
Hope-Taylor
1987, Ferrell
1990 and
Tinniswood &
Harding 1991.)

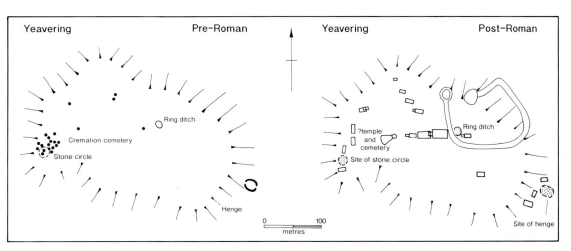

In the post-Roman period it seems as if a selection of these sites were brought back into use after an interval of perhaps 2,000 years during which many of them had apparently been forgotten. But if their importance had lapsed, their earthworks certainly survived. We can see these developments at two geographical scales, and it is my submission that they were so pervasive that, taken together, they invested the landscape as a whole with a new layer of meaning. At the same time, they associated the political developments of the day with a history and a range of associations that had little justification in reality.

Individual monuments were certainly reused, and occasionally they were recreated. The timber buildings at Yeavering not only extended between two of the prehistoric monuments on the site: both earthworks could have been purposefully rebuilt (Hope-Taylor 1977, 70–8, 108–16; illus 60). It is hard to be sure how many of the prehistoric monuments were still visible, but an older mound or ring ditch seems to have been encapsulated in the defences of a fort. Whether by accident or design, its position was marked by an enormous post. The stone circle at the opposite end of the complex was replaced by a pagan temple, then both monuments were chosen for the creation of cemeteries. The same was true in the landscape at large, for two of the henges close to the royal complex at Milfield were treated in much the same way (Scull & Harding 1990). In one case it is not certain that this juxtaposition was intended, but on the other site the distribution of graves was defined by the surviving bank of the enclosure.

At a broader level it seems as if the original layout of the ceremonial centre was recreated in the post-Roman period (illus 61). The original row of henge monu-

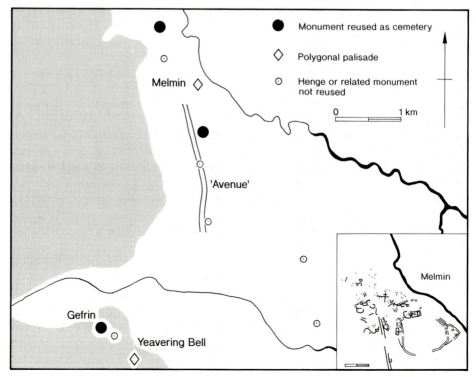

61
The distribution of early medieval sites in the Milfield Basin, with a detail of the cropmarks of Melmin. (Data from Bradley 1987b and Scull & Harding 1990.)

ments appears to have been enhanced by a double-ditched 'avenue' linking three of the sites and leading into the royal centre at Milfield. Two of the enclosures joined in this new design were associated with post-Roman burials (*ibid*). This avenue has been treated as an early feature (Harding 1981, 89–93), but it seems to post-date the individual enclosures and appropriate parallels are completely lacking in the prehistoric period. In view of its close link with the Milfield palace complex, the best comparison might be with the 'royal roadways' associated with high status sites in early medieval Ireland (Wailes 1982). As I mentioned earlier, a number of the henges were directed towards prominent features of the skyline, including the distinctive peak of Yeavering Bell. This emphasis on alignments between the sites seems less surprising when we find that a palisaded enclosure, very likely of this date, was built on the mountaintop. Its position encapsulates another complicated history, for it was superimposed on the position of some of the houses within an older hillfort (Bradley 1987b, 10).

◆ ◆ ◆

Although Bede's account sheds light on the identification of the sites at Yeavering and Milfield, it tells us all too little about their wider associations. My second example provides some compensation. This time I am concerned with the reuse of Neolithic monuments in the Boyne Valley. Again they were discussed in the previous lecture. All three of the largest tombs saw a phase of renewed activity during the first millennium AD, but at Dowth too little survives for this evidence to be drawn into a wider interpretation (O'Kelly & O'Kelly 1983). For that reason I shall concern myself with the changing history of the neighbouring mounds of Knowth and Newgrange. In this case we have a rare opportunity of comparing the evidence from modern excavations with the traditional associations of both these monuments (O'Kelly 1982; Eogan 1986; 1991).

These tombs play different roles in the early history of Ireland (illus 62). During its heyday Knowth was one of the focal points of a small kingdom, the northern Brega. It was a royal capital (Byrne 1968), and excavation has confirmed its importance as a high status settlement. Early in the first millennium AD it was enclosed by two concentric earthworks which transformed the Neolithic mound into a massive ring fort. Around its base were nearly forty burials, some of them associated with an unusually rich collection of grave goods (Eogan 1991); a similar arrangement is found around the Ulster passage tomb of Kiltierney (Hamlin & Lynn 1988, 124–6). In contrast to Knowth, Newgrange was always viewed as a tomb, as the burial place of the ancestors, the dwelling of supernatural beings (O'Kelly 1982). That interpretation was no doubt supported by the way in which the midwinter sunrise lit its central chamber.

Again, there is an archaeological counterpart to the legendary history of Newgrange, for scattered around the periphery of the mound, and in particular towards its entrance, is some of the finest Roman metalwork found in Ireland (Carson & O'Kelly 1977). Similar collections are rare but a few pieces are known from Knowth, and there are more from other high status sites such as Tara (Warner 1976). The collection from Newgrange has a distinctive composition.

The artefacts had been carefully selected and must have been deposited intention-ally. The most likely explanation is that they were intended as offerings. But offer-ings to whom?

In fact there seems to be a clear relationship between the legendary history of Newgrange and the archaeological sequence at Knowth, where excavation charts its changing role in Irish history. At first the ancestors of the local rulers were cred-ited with supernatural powers and were thought to live inside the mound at Newgrange (O'Kelly 1982). The finds of Roman metalwork may have been dedic-ated to them, and their association with this site helped to confirm the legitimacy of the political system. When the settlement at Knowth was absorbed into a larger unit, the history of Newgrange was revised. Far from being the home of the gods, it was the burial place of the High Kings of Ireland. Its past was reinterpreted to fit changing political circumstances (Byrne 1968; O'Kelly 1982).

In this case we are able to combine two distinct lines of argument – archaeology and legend – to show how prehistoric monuments could be used to legitimise a political elite and to lend it the authority of the past. But it is very rare to be able to trace these processes in so much detail. For every Yeavering or Knowth, there are other sites where the archaeological sequence poses problems and historical

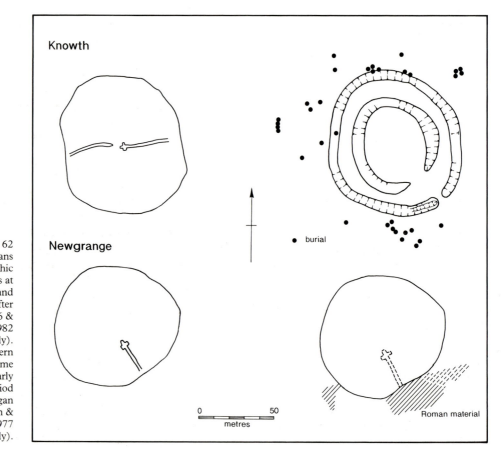

62
(Left) Outline plans of the Neolithic passage tombs at Knowth and Newgrange (after Eogan 1986 & O'Kelly 1982 respectively). (Right) The pattern of reuse at the same sites during the early historical period (data from Eogan 1991 and Carson & O'Kelly 1977 respectively).

sources are silent. In such cases it would be all too easy to let the argument lapse, but there are certain gains in working at a large geographical scale. If the evidence of individual monuments is often insubstantial, can any general trends be discerned at a regional level? Again I shall take my examples from the early post-Roman period.

In most areas our starting point is the end of the Western Roman empire. This has been studied most systematically on the Continent, where the evidence for the continued use of Roman sites has been carefully assessed. In particular, there are useful studies of the turnover of urban buildings and the maintenance of different kinds of Roman structure, from houses and fortifications to temples and public works (Ward-Perkins 1984; Greenhalgh 1989). The British Isles, on the other hand, exhibit a far more varied pattern, and it is this legacy that I wish to consider now. How far did the selection of particular sites for reuse, or, alternatively, their rejection in favour of other locations, diverge along regional lines? And if it did so, what light can it shed on the ways in which different societies in the post-Roman world constructed their own histories?

The British Isles were at the extreme edge of the Roman empire, but its official limits fluctuated though time. We can see this even in terms of modern geographical divisions. England was largely assimilated into the Roman system, although there were certainly limits to that process in the north and along the Atlantic seaboard. Wales, on the other hand, was essentially a military zone in which the Romans never secured a firm hold. Towns and villas are uncommon and the most massive constructions are the forts. Scotland shares this characteristic, but with a significant difference, for in this case the extent of Roman power fluctuated between and beyond the frontiers. This was an area in which experience of the Roman world will have varied from one period to another. Lastly, although political contacts certainly existed, Ireland remained outside that sphere of influence completely, and when we find Roman imports, as we do at Newgrange or Tara, they seem to have played a part in an entirely different social system.

These different histories are obvious in the archaeological record and have been discussed on many occasions. Less obvious perhaps, but almost equally revealing, are the ways in which those pasts were used after the Roman collapse. Here again we can combine some of the archaeological evidence with the evidence of literary tradition. But it would be quite misleading to consider this material in relation to modern political divisions. As we have already seen, there is only a partial overlap between national boundaries and the extent and character of Roman power. It is much more revealing to try to recognise different types of transition in the archaeological evidence, and only then to consider how far they characterise separate parts of the British Isles.

Let us start with the evidence from the urban core of Roman Britain. Here opinion has shown a significant shift during recent years, from a belief that Roman towns remained in use into the historical period to a growing acceptance that they were

abandoned, even if they were reoccupied later (Esmonde-Cleary 1989). The demise of those towns occurred at different paces, and there are certainly instances in which archaeological and historical evidence shows that some of their functions remained intact after the formal withdrawal of Roman power. Even so, the strongest evidence for the continued importance of towns comes from two distinct sources, both of them essentially new. Certain towns, such as Canterbury, seem to have become important ecclesiastical centres with a significant role in the administration of the Christian church. Perhaps the strongest archaeological evidence comes from Lincoln where the church of St Paul in the Bail was located at the centre of the Roman forum, whose imposing remains must have provided a monumental backcloth to the new construction (Steane 1992). The archaeological sequence remains to be resolved, but the discovery of a hanging bowl inside this building provides a purely insular component of the equation.

A similar situation may have arisen at late Roman forts like Burgh Castle which were selected as the sites of monasteries (Johnson 1983). As Michael Hunter (1974) points out, the very act of Christian baptism invoked connections with the imperial past, for often it was undertaken by foreign missionaries and took place in major Roman towns. Somewhat later, in the Middle Saxon period, such towns may have been at least as important as the bases of Christian kings. Both the church and some of the royal dynasties looked to Continental Europe, and particularly to the successors of the Roman state, as a source of legitimate authority (Moreland & Van de Noort 1992). On the other hand, in neither case can we show clear evidence for the continued nucleation of population or for the sheer range of productive activities that had characterised their use in Roman times.

That is not to deny the scale of craft production or the importance of long distance trade (Hodges 1982). The international significance of a number of coastal sites has long been known from historical sources, but until recently it seemed impossible to reconcile these with any convincing body of archaeological material. That even applies to such a famous site as London, where the historical evidence for occupation seemed to be contradicted by signs of a period of desertion between the late Roman and late Saxon periods. In fact, recent fieldwork in several towns has revealed a striking pattern spanning part of that period. From about AD 700 those towns were indeed in use and participated in large scale production and exchange, but they did so from locations some way outside the limits of their Roman predecessors. That pattern has now been recognised at London (Hobley 1988), Southampton (Brisbane 1988) and York (Kemp, R 1987) and it calls for more discussion than it has received so far. There is little to suggest that one location was more suitable than another, and in fact the movement away from the surviving fabric of the Roman towns may signify a rejection of the past. That might also be consistent with the cultural axis of the early trade routes, which extended far beyond the frontiers of the Romanised world. It was only through the quite different alignment of the Christian church that some sense of a Roman inheritance was maintained, and it was surely from that starting point that the re-emergence of older towns began. When that happened, the process was most obvious in lowland England.

As so often, there are some special cases, and it is certainly true that a combination of archaeological and traditional sources suggest that a small number of towns or forts may have been associated with powerful groups or individuals in the wake of the Roman collapse. Possible examples include the towns at Wroxeter, Catterick and Caerwent, and possibly the forts of Segontium, Pen Llystyn and Birdoswald. None of the evidence is clear-cut but it does have certain common properties. A palisaded enclosure overlies the fort at Pen Llystyn (Hogg 1968) and massive halls were built over the Roman ruins at Birdoswald (Wilmott 1989). At Wroxeter, the central area of the town was replanned after the public buildings had gone out of use (Barker, P 1975). In other cases there are finds of early post-Roman artefacts (Edwards & Lane 1988). Little of this material commands much confidence, for where the archaeological contexts are well documented, the chronological evidence is weak, whilst the best dated artefacts are essentially unprovenanced. Here we have to rely on the additional support of historical evidence which suggests that a number of these places could have been associated with leaders in the early post-Roman world (Alcock 1987). The evidence from western Britain is particularly interesting because Magnus Maximus plays a significant part in early Welsh genealogy. Equally important, these sites are all found around the limits of the Roman province, and there may even be historical links between post-Roman society in Wales and northern England.

Hints of even more local distinctions can be found elsewhere in the frontier zone. Martin Biddle has pointed out that early churches are associated with Roman forts along the western section of Hadrian's Wall (1976, 67). In the eastern half, they avoid those monuments entirely. He suggests that the division corresponds with the territories of two different groups: the Britons of Strathclyde to the west and the Votadini to the east. The contrast may be due to different attitudes to the Roman world and to the adoption of Christianity. The argument is an attractive one but it needs testing by excavation.

I mentioned that western Britain had never been fully assimilated into the Roman system. The same point is illustrated by the later history of Roman sites in that area. Of particular importance is the extent to which late Roman and early post-Roman material has been discovered at older hillforts. This may be linked with the creation of Romano-Celtic temples in the countryside and, in southwest England, with the establishment of late Roman cemeteries in these locations (Rahtz & Watts 1979). One possibility is that we are witnessing the re-establishment of an older, decentralised pattern represented by prehistoric hillforts. It may have grown up in competition with the urban settlements, and these are the sites that went on in use into the post-Roman period when occupation of the nearby towns came to an end. There is nothing new in an interpretation which sees a reciprocal relationship between late Roman use of the towns and the growth of hilltop settlement (Burrow 1981). I would merely add the rider that the use of such locations for hillforts, shrines and even cemeteries might be part of a revival of traditional practice, half remembered and half invented. At all events it signalled the rejection of urban life.

The same pattern is seen at sites in Wales and Scotland, where hilltop temples are lacking. In this case it would be wrong to emphasise the contrast with Roman practice quite so sharply, for some of the new centres of power were well away from any Roman forts. But one striking pattern is worth mentioning here. On at least three sites with well-attested post-Roman ramparts, Ruberslaw and Clatchard Craig in Scotland (Curle 1905; Close-Brooks 1986) and South Cadbury in south-west England (Alcock 1982), it seems as if a deliberate decision was taken to incorporate Roman building material in the defences. Although this could have been found near to South Cadbury, in the other cases it seems to have been brought in from a distance, in one case from the Roman fort of Carpow. This suggests a distinctly ambivalent attitude to the Roman inheritance: the fort itself was shunned and yet some of the building material was transported to a quite different location, where it was of no particular use. It seems possible that a similar attitude to the past is evidenced at other sites. At Cadbury Congresbury the excavators have argued that Roman artefacts were introduced to the fortified settlement long after they had gone out of commission; once there, these objects were deposited with some formality (Burrow 1981, ch 6). Peter Hill (1987) has recently suggested that the same interpretation applies to the Roman metalwork from Traprain Law.

Earlier, I mentioned the remarkable site of Yeavering close to the Scottish border, but so far I have confined myself to the way in which its Neolithic and Bronze Age monuments were reused during the post-Roman period. There is one extraordinary building at Yeavering which is quite separate from these prehistoric earthworks. This is the timber amphitheatre on the site (Hope-Taylor 1977), which can only have been inspired by Roman prototypes, although none had been built for well over a century; in any case the most obvious sources of inspiration are in areas well to the south of Hadrian's Wall. It is difficult to say much about a structure which lacks any obvious parallel, but the reference to the Roman inheritance is clear, although the builders of Yeavering may have been alone in constructing a past out of so many disparate elements.

———————————— ◆◆◆ ————————————

For the most part, the sites which make reference to Roman buildings or material culture are around the outer edges of the province, in south-west England or close to the northern frontier. In some ways Yeavering and Milfield are rather unusual, for the reuse of earlier prehistoric monuments is generally found in more distant areas; the one exception is the relatively late site at Thwing on the Yorkshire Wolds (Manby 1986). The best known evidence for the reuse of prehistoric monuments comes from Ireland, but it can be misunderstood in much the same way as the archaeological sequence at Yeavering. There is no doubt that some of the Irish royal sites do have features in common with Neolithic monuments. Certain of the major enclosures can be compared with henges, just as the timber settings inside them recall the structures found within Late Neolithic enclosures, from eastern Scotland to Wessex (Wailes 1982, 19–20). The problem is that good Irish precedents are lacking, whilst the sites which show the strongest resemblances to one another are separated by 2,000 years.

One approach is to postulate the continuous existence of ritual specialists – Druids are the favourite candidates – who maintained traditional learning across the generations (cf MacKie 1977, 229). There are serious objections to this idea. Irish henge monuments are poorly dated and do not resemble their counterparts on the mainland especially closely. The great timber settings of the royal sites have a more convincing source among the Late Bronze Age ringworks in Ireland, particularly Navan (cf Cooney & Grogan 1991). Yet the fact remains that an unexpectedly high proportion of the royal centres did occupy important Neolithic sites. I have already discussed the sequence at Knowth; an equally convincing example is found at Tara (O'Riordain 1959). The main elements to attract attention, however, were not enclosures but mounds. This seems hardly surprising when we consider that some of the major passage tombs in Ireland carried elaborate decoration and in several cases adopted obvious astronomical alignments. At present there is no real evidence that Irish henge monuments were brought back into use, although Derek Simpson (1989) has suggested that the outer enclosure at Navan could be a Neolithic monument. A Neolithic structure of some kind may also have existed at the centre of Dún Ailinne (Wailes 1990).

In fact some of the major complexes have a longer history than either Yeavering or Knowth, where there was a considerable interval between the use of the prehistoric monuments and their recreation in the first millennium AD. At Tara, for example, rich Early Bronze Age burials were inserted into the Neolithic passage tomb that was the oldest structure on the site, and fine metalwork of Later Bronze Age origin was found nearby (O'Riordain 1959); two gold hoards of similar date come from Downpatrick, where the full archaeological sequence is uncertain (Proudfoot 1955; 1957). There may be other sites with a more varied history. At Rathcroghan the evidence takes a different form, and here the earthworks include mortuary mounds that could span the entire prehistoric sequence (Waddell 1988). In a few cases the associations of royal centres may be less apparent from their surface topography. At least one of these sites seems to have developed at what we can call an offering place. This is the royal crannog of Lagore, which overlay a complex sequence of deposits that have never been studied systematically (Hencken 1950). They included a deer skeleton, animal bones, items of Bronze Age metalwork, human bones including a skull and a remarkable wood sculpture dated by radiocarbon to about 2000 BC (Coles 1990, 322–3, 326). At one time the crannog itself was the capital of the southern Brega and would have been the counterpart of its northern capital at Knowth.

I have argued that mounds like Knowth were particularly attractive in the selection of royal sites in Ireland. The same point can be illustrated by the excavated earth-works at Clogher (Warner 1988). But the reuse of older mounds is by no means restricted to Ireland. Steven Driscoll has recently drawn attention to the importance of 'those ceremonial centres which served as meeting places, the places to hold popular courts and the sites of quasi-religious inaugurations to high office' (1991, 98). As he says, the best known of these is Moot Hill at Scone. There are several cases in which such sites can be identified through place names and appear to be associated with prehistoric earthworks, cairns and settings of stones. In his own study area one such site seems to be marked by the position of a causewayed enclosure and a henge, whilst a more famous example is found at Forteviot where Leslie Alcock has been working. In this case the importance of a Pictish royal

centre is attested by several different sources: historical accounts, monumental sculptures and a carved stone arch (Alcock 1984, 28–9). The site has probably been identified from the air, but for our purposes it is significant that near to it are the crop marks of a Neolithic enclosure, as well as several small henge monuments and mounds. Interspersed among them are the sites of square barrows probably dating from the first millennium AD.

Such sites as Forteviot and Tara seem to show a similar attitude to the remains of the past and developed in relation to monument complexes of Neolithic and Early Bronze Age date. It is a sequence that is perhaps best established in Ireland, but it can be recognised more widely; yet there seems to be no need to postulate detailed links between different areas. What they do share is a remoteness from the Roman system and a willingness to ground political developments in a different and more remote past. It may be true that in England and Scotland the people who created these centres had little appreciation of the antiquity of the surviving remains, but that hardly matters. What they could appreciate was that they were entirely distinct from the relics of Roman colonisation.

I am coming close to the territory mapped out with much greater expertise in Leslie Alcock's Rhind Lectures (Alcock 1988), and this might seem the ideal point at which to close. But I do have one more suggestion to make, and in doing so I shall take us back full circle to my starting point on the rock of Dunadd. So far I have said nothing about the extraordinary natural appearance of many of the high status centres of the early post-Roman period, those fortified crags that Leslie Alcock has made so much his own. These are distributed far more widely than the other sites I have considered, and for the most part they lack the same association with older monuments. Among the features that seem to unite them are their distinctive natural setting. To a prehistorian like myself these places look very much alike. Who could deny the striking physical presence – indeed, the similar appearance – of Tintagel, the Rock of Cashel or the Mote of Mark (illus 63)? To quote Professor Alcock's discussion of three of these sites (Dumbarton, Dunadd and Dundurn):

> 'What links these three major Celtic strongholds is not the plans of their defences, but the stepped topography of the hills on which they were set. The hill was primary, the defences secondary, and the close relationship of hill and defences was something which evolved with time. The particular significance of the slope of the hill was that it lent itself to a hierarchical organisation of space' (Alcock *et al* 1989, 210).

It lent itself to that distinctive layout, but it made it seem natural at the same time.

I wonder whether there is still another dimension, for as I said at the beginning of this lecture, the visual effect of such sites makes them quintessentially places that have been transformed into monuments. We cannot offer much evidence of their remoter history, but it does seem most unlikely that they lacked all mythical assoc-

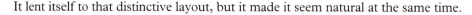

iations until the very moment when they were first defended. They may be works of nature, but they were also places which could have evoked a range of complex responses that are lost to field archaeology. And in that sense they were beyond time itself.

I started at Dunadd, and I shall end there, for that site and the archaeology of the area around it provide concrete examples of practically everything that I have suggested in these lectures (illus 64). I do not say this merely as a literary device, as a way of rooting these thoughts in the Scottish experience. What I have discussed are a series of ideas that grow out of the experience of visiting and thinking about monuments. Ideally, a study of this kind would work best if it could be grounded in the archaeology of just a single area – even of a single site – developing different ways of coming to terms with its history. At present I do not think that this is possible, although there are areas like Orkney where this objective may soon be within our grasp. I have had to follow a more devious course, drawing out several lines of thought that were suggested by the monuments of Mid Argyll, but developing these at different geographical scales according to the quality of the archaeological evidence and the limits of my own knowledge. As often as not, that led me to consider the prehistory of Continental Europe, but in this final lecture I have returned entirely to the archaeology of the British Isles.

Even on a continental scale the British landscape is extraordinary for the extent to which prehistoric monuments survive. At their best there is little to match their abundance and sheer variety. Yet I would contend that there are lessons still to be learned if we are to study them effectively. We no longer investigate the ancient pattern of settlement through the piecemeal recording of occupation sites. Where possible, we work at a larger scale, linking the separate settlements to their boundaries, their field systems and to the wider use

63
The Mote of Mark, Dumfries and Galloway.

of the terrain. That is the lesson of the recent Royal Commission survey of north-east Perth (RCAHMS 1990). But we have yet to appreciate how necessary it is to treat the more specialised monuments in a similar frame of mind: to consider their relationship with one another and the patterns of interpretation and cross-reference that inform us of the mental world they once inhabited. As with landscape archaeology, the right time scale is one of centuries, if not millennia, but unlike settlements and field systems, the more prominent monuments of earlier prehistory – enclosures, stone settings, mounds and decorated rocks – impose themselves on human consciousness in most distinctive ways. We recognise that as consumers of the human past, and some of us contend with just that dimension as the managers of what survives. The paradox is that we have become so skilled at explaining settlement patterns at a time when the public show more concern with questions that we feel reluctant to answer. For every settlement or field system that we can explain, at least to our own satisfaction, there are more conspicuous monuments that we find entirely enigmatic. Perhaps that is because we have always taken them for granted. For that very reason they pose their challenge now.

64
Dunadd and the
surrounding
landscape.
Photograph:
Historic Scotland.

When we visit an area like Mid Argyll, we are confronted with just how different the past was from the present. It is this feeling of difference that we would do so well to emphasise in our work. In the first lecture I argued that we tend to create a

past in terms that are familiar to us, to explain the archaeology of monuments though the assumptions of an agricultural society like our own. In the second, I went on to argue that we overlook the wider significance of place in an unmapped landscape, and I returned to that point when I discussed the post-Roman occupation of sites like Dunadd. Because we lack that ability to incorporate the unaltered topography into our sense of the landscape, we have marginalised whole areas of archaeological fieldwork. That is why, for instance, rock art has played little part in mainstream prehistory. But, as I suggested in the third lecture, monuments and places worked together to direct and stimulate the experience of prehistoric people. It is their inability to come to terms with experience itself that leaves prehistorians so vulnerable to the inroads of alternative archaeologies.

Last of all, monuments feed off the associations, not only of places, but also of other monuments. Monuments are enhanced and rebuilt; they are reinterpreted and changed; and new constructions are created around old ones. We tend to lose that dimension of the archaeological record as we become immersed in chronological analysis. In their different ways the last three lectures have all had points in common. What we think of as the evolution of monuments, their ordering according to a linear perception of time, was really a process of finding out about the world: a way in which successive generations established a sense of place and time in relation to the living and the dead. On occasion this involved the wholesale rejection of monuments, their abandonment or destruction. At others, it required a greater act of the imagination: a process of recreating a past that was really beyond recall and of making it play an unrehearsed part in the present.

That is also what archaeologists do. It is what I was doing as I walked through the prehistory of Mid Argyll two years ago. And it is what our public do when they visit those same places. Our perceptions are bound to be different, but we should be able to talk to one another. More than anything else, the archaeology of monuments is where those conversations begin.

REFERENCES

Abélanet, J 1986 *Signes sans paroles*. Paris: Hachette.

Alcock, L 1982 'Cadbury–Camelot: a fifteen year perspective', *Proc British Acad*, 68 (1982), 355–88.

Alcock, L 1984 'A survey of Pictish settlement archaeology', *in* Friell, J & Watson, W (eds), *Pictish Studies*, 7–41. Oxford: BAR. (= *BAR Brit Ser*, 125.)

Alcock, L 1987 *Economy, society and warfare among the Britons and Saxons*. Cardiff: Univ Wales Press.

Alcock, L 1988 'The Rhind Lectures 1988–89: a synopsis. An heroic age: war and society in northern Britain', *Proc Soc Antiq Scot*, 118 (1988), 327–34.

Alcock, L, Alcock, E & Driscoll, S 1989 'Reconnaissance excavations on Early Historic fortifications and other royal sites in Scotland, 1974–84: 3, Excavations at Dundurn, Strathearn, Perthshire, 1976–77', *Proc Soc Antiq Scot*, 119 (1989), 189–226, fiche 2:A2–3:E11.

Ammerman, A & Cavalli-Sforza, L 1984 *The Neolithic transition and the genetics of populations in Europe*. Princeton: Princeton Univ Press.

Anati, E (ed) 1976a *Les Gravures Protohistoriques dans les Alpes*. Nice: Union Internationale des Sciences Préhistoriques et Protohistoriques.

Anati, E 1976b *Evolution and style in Camunan rock art*. Capo da Ponte: Centro Camuno di Studi Preistorici.

Andersen, N 1988 'Sarup: two Neolithic enclosures in south-west Funen', *J Danish Archaeol*, 7 (1988), 93–114.

Arnal, J 1973 'Le Lébous à Saint-Mathieu-de-Treviers (Hérault), ensemble du Chalcolithique au Gallo-Romain. 1: Etude Archéologique', *Gallia Préhist*, 16 (1973), 131–93.

Atkinson R, Piggott, CM & Sandars, N 1951 *Excavations at Dorchester, Oxon*. Oxford: Ashmolean Mus.

Auden, WH 1940 'Spain 1937', *in* Auden, WH, *Another time*, 103–6. London: Faber and Faber.

Bahn, P 1984 *Pyrenean prehistory*. Warminster: Aris & Phillips.

Bakker, JA 1979 *The West TRB group*. Amsterdam: Cingula 5.

Barfield, L 1986 'Chalcolithic burial ritual in Northern Italy: problems of interpretation', *Dialoghi di Archeologia*, 2 (1986), 241–8.

Barker, G 1985 *Prehistoric farming in Europe*. Cambridge: Cambridge Univ Press.

Barker, P 1975 'Excavations on the site of the Baths-Basilica at Wroxeter 1966–74: an interim report', *Britannia*, 6 (1975), 106–17.

Barnatt, J 1989 *Stone Circles of Britain*. Oxford: BAR. (= *BAR Brit Ser*, 215.)

Barrett, J in press *Fragments from antiquity: the archaeology of social life in Britain, 2900–1200 BC*. Oxford: Blackwell.

Barrett, J, Bradley, R & Green, M 1991 *Landscape, monuments and society. The prehistory of Cranborne Chase.* Cambridge: Cambridge Univ Press.

Beckensall, S 1992 *Cumbrian prehistoric rock art: symbols, monuments and landscape.* Hexham: privately published.

Bender, B 1985 'Prehistoric developments in the American midcontinent and in Brittany, north-west France', *in* Price, TD & Brown, J (eds), *Prehistoric hunter gatherers: the emergence of cultural complexity*, 21–57. New York: Academic Press.

Bender, B 1989 'The roots of inequality', *in* Miller, D, Rowlands, M & Tilley, C (eds), *Domination and Resistance*, 83–95. London: Unwin Hyman.

Biddle, M 1976 'The archaeology of the church: a widening horizon', *in* Addyman, P & Morris, R (eds), *The archaeological study of churches*, 65–71. London: CBA. (= *CBA Res Rep*, 13).

Bird-David, N 1990 'The giving environment: another perspective on the economic system of gatherer-hunters', *Current Anthropol*, 31 (1990), 189–96.

Bird-David, N 1992 'Beyond "The original affluent society": a culturalist reformulation', *Current Anthropol*, 33 (1992), 25–47.

Bloch, M 1989 *Ritual, history and power.* London: Athlone Press.

Boelicke, U 1976 'Das Neolithische Erdwerk Urmitz', *Acta Praehistorica et Archaeologica*, 7 (1976), 73–121.

Boelicke, U, Van Brandt, D, Lüning, J, Stehli, P & Zimmerman, A 1988 *Der bandkeramische Siedlungplatz Langweiler 8.* Bonn: Habelt.

Bonnanno, A, Gouder, T, Malone, C & Stoddart, S 1990 'Monuments in an island society: the Maltese context', *World Archaeol*, 22 (1990), 190–205.

Bowen, HC 1990 *The Archaeology of Bokerley Dyke.* London: HMSO.

Bradley, R 1975 'Maumbury Rings, Dorchester – the excavations of 1908–13', *Archaeologia*, 105 (1975), 1–97.

Bradley, R 1981 'From ritual to romance: ceremonial enclosures and hillforts', *in* Guilbert, G (ed), *Hillfort Studies*, 20–27. Leicester: Leicester Univ Press.

Bradley, R 1987a 'Flint technology and the character of Neolithic settlement', *in* Brown, A & Edmonds, M (eds), *Lithic analysis and later British prehistory*, 181–5. Oxford: BAR. (= *BAR Brit Ser*, 162).

Bradley, R 1987b 'Time regained – the creation of continuity', *J Brit Archaeol Assoc*, 140 (1987), 1–17.

Bradley, R 1990 *The passage of arms. An archaeological analysis of prehistoric hoards and votive deposits.* Cambridge: Cambridge Univ Press.

Bradley, R 1991 'Rock art and the perception of landscape', *Cambridge Archaeol J*, 1 (1991), 77–101.

Bradley, R 1992 'Turning the world: rock carvings and the archaeology of death', *in* Sharples, N & Sheridan, A (eds), *Vessels for the ancestors*, 168–76. Edinburgh: Edinburgh Univ Press.

Bradley, R in press 'The excavation of an oval barrow beside the Abingdon causewayed enclosure', *Proc Prehist Soc*, 58.

Bradley, R & Chambers, R 1988 'A new study of the cursus complex at Dorchester on Thames', *Oxford J Archaeol*, 7 (1988), 271–89.

Bradley, R & Edmonds, M in press *Interpreting the axe trade. Production and exchange in Neolithic Britain.* Cambridge: Cambridge Univ Press.

Bradley, R, Meredith, P, Smith, J & Edmonds, M 1992 'Rock physics and the Neolithic axe trade in Great Britain', *Archaeometry*, 34 (1992), 223–33.

Briard, J 1989 *Mégalithes de Haute Bretagne*. Paris: Editions de la Maison des Sciences de l'Homme.

Brisbane, M 1988 'Hamwic (Saxon Southampton): an eighth-century port and production centre', *in* Hodges, R & Hobley, B (eds), *The rebirth of towns in the West, AD 700–1000*, 10–18. London: CBA. (= *CBA Res Rep*, 68.)

Burgess, C 1990 'The chronology of cup- and cup-and-ring marks in Atlantic Europe', *in* Monnier, J (ed), *La Bretagne et l'Europe préhistorique*, 157–71. Rennes: Revue Archéologique de l'Ouest, Supplément 2.

Burkill, M 1984 'The Middle Neolithic of the Paris Basin', *in* Scarre, C (ed), *Ancient France*, 34–61. Edinburgh: Edinburgh Univ Press.

Burl, A 1976 *The stone circles of the British Isles*. New Haven: Yale Univ Press.

Burl, A 1987 *The Stonehenge people*. London: Dent.

Burl, A 1991 *Prehistoric henges*. Princes Risborough: Shire Publications.

Burrow, I 1981 *Hillfort and hilltop settlement in Somerset in the first to eighth centuries AD*. Oxford: BAR. (= *BAR Brit Ser*, 91.)

Buttler, W & Haberey, W 1936 *Die bandkeramische Ansiedlung bei Köln-Lindenthal*. Leipzig: Römisch-Germanisches Kommission.

Byrne, FJ 1968 'Historical note on Cnogba (Knowth)', *Proc Roy Ir Acad C*, 66 (1968), 383–400.

Camps, G 1988 *Préhistoire d'une île. Les origines de la Corse*. Paris: Errance.

Carson, R & O'Kelly, C 1977 'A catalogue of the Roman coins from Newgrange, Co Meath, and notes on the coins and related finds', *Proc Roy Ir Acad C*, 77 (1977), 35–55.

Case, H 1969 'Neolithic explanations', *Antiquity*, 43 (1969), 176–86.

Chapman, R 1981 'The emergence of formal disposal areas and the "problem" of megalithic tombs in prehistoric Europe', *in* Chapman, R, Kinnes, I & Randsborg, K (eds), *The archaeology of death*, 71–82. Cambridge: Cambridge Univ Press.

Chenorkian, R 1988 *Les armes métalliques dans l'art protohistorique de l'occident Méditerranéen*. Paris: Editions du Centre National de la Recherche Scientifique.

Clark, G & Neely, M 1987 'Social differentiation in European Mesolithic burial data', *in* Rowley-Conwy, P, Zvelebil, M & Blankholm, H (eds), *Mesolithic north-west Europe: recent trends*, 121–7. Sheffield: Univ Sheffield Dept Archaeol Prehist.

Cleal, R 1991 'Cranborne Chase – the earlier prehistoric pottery', *in* Barrett, J, Bradley, R, & Hall, M (eds) *Papers on the prehistoric archaeology of Cranborne Chase*, 134–200. Oxford: Oxbow Books.

Close-Brooks, J 1986 'Excavations at Clatchard Craig, Fife', *Proc Soc Antiq Scot*, 116 (1986), 117–84, fiche 1:B1–C14.

Cohen, A 1985 *The symbolic construction of community*. London: Tavistock Publications.

Coles, B 1990 'Anthropomorphic wooden figurines from Britain and Ireland', *Proc Prehist Soc*, 56 (1990), 315–33.

Colomer, A 1979 *Les grottes sépulchrales artificielles en Languedoc orientale*. Toulouse: Ecole des Hautes Etudes en Sciences Sociales.

Connerton, P 1989 *How societies remember*. Cambridge: Cambridge Univ Press.

Cooney, G & Grogan, E 1991 'An archaeological solution to the "Irish" problem?', *Emainia*, 9 (1991), 33–43.

Coudart, A & Demoule, JP 1982 'Le site néolithique et chalcolithique de Menneville', *Rev Archéol de Picardie*, numéro spécial (1982), 119–47.

Craw, J 1931 'Further excavations of cairns at Poltalloch, Argyll', *Proc Soc Antiq Scot*, 65 (1930–1), 269–80.

Criado Boado, F 1989a 'We the post-megalithic people', *in* Hodder, I (ed), *The meanings of things*, 79–89. London: Unwin Hyman.

Criado Boado, F 1989b 'Megaliticos, espacio, pensiamento', *Trabajos de Prehistoria*, 46 (1989), 75–98.

Curle, A 1905 'Description of the fortifications on Ruberslaw, Roxburghshire', *Proc Soc Antiq Scot*, 39 (1904–5), 219–32.

Curwen, EC 1931 'Excavations at the Trundle. Second season, 1930', *Sussex Archaeol Collect*, 72 (1931), 100–49.

D'Anna, A 1977 *Les statues-menhirs et stèles anthropomorphes du Midi Mediterranéen*. Paris: Editions du Centre National de la Recherche Scientifique.

De Lumley, H, Fontvielle, M & Abélanet, J 1976 'Les gravures rupestres de l'âge du Bronze dans la région du Mont-Bégo', *in* Guilaine, J (ed), *La préhistoire Française*, 222–36. Paris: Editions du Centre Nationale de la Recherche Scientifique.

Dent, J 1982 'Cemeteries and settlement patterns of the Iron Age on the Yorkshire Wolds', *Proc Prehist Soc*, 48 (1982), 437–57.

Driscoll, S 1991 'The archaeology of state formation in Scotland', *in* Hanson, W & Slater, E (eds), *Scottish archaeology: new perceptions*, 81–111. Aberdeen: Aberdeen Univ Press.

Dubouloz, J, Ilett, M & Lasserre, M 1982 'Enceintes et maisons chalcolithiques de Berry-au-Bac, La Croix Maigret (Aisne)', *in La Néolithique de l'est de la France*, 193–206. Chalons-sur-Marne: Soc Archéol de Sens.

Edwards, N & Lane, A 1988 *Early Medieval settlements in Wales, AD 400–1100*. Cardiff: Cardiff Univ Dept Archaeol.

Emmett, D 1979 'Stone rows: the traditional view reconsidered', *Proc Devon Archaeol Soc*, 37 (1979), 94–114.

Eogan, G 1986 *Knowth and the passage-tombs of Ireland*. London: Thames & Hudson.

Eogan, G 1991 'Prehistoric and early historic culture change at Brugh na Bóinne', *Proc Roy Ir Acad C*, 91 (1991), 105–32.

Esmonde-Cleary, AS 1989 *The ending of Roman Britain*. London: Batsford.

Evans, C 1989 'Digging with the pen', *Archaeol Rev Cambridge*, 8.2 (1989), 185–212.

Ferrell, G 1990 'A reassessment of the prehistoric pottery from the 1952 excavations at Yeavering', *Archaeol Aeliana*, 18, 29–49.

Finnegan, R 1977 *Oral poetry*. Cambridge: Cambridge Univ Press.

Fischer, A 1982 'Trade in Neolithic shaft-hole axes and the introduction of Neolithic economy', *J Danish Archaeol*, 1 (1982), 7–12.

Fleming, A 1988 *The Dartmoor reaves*. London: Batsford.

Flood, J 1980 *The moth eaters*. Canberra: Inst Aboriginal Stud.

Flood, J 1989 *Archaeology of the dreamtime*. 2 edn. Sydney: Collins.

Ford, J & Webb, C 1956 'Poverty Point – a late archaic site in Louisiana', *Washington: American Mus Natur Hist Anthropol Pap*, 46 (1956), 1–136.

Fulford, M 1989 *The Silchester amphitheatre: excavations of 1979–85*. London: Soc Promotion Roman Stud. (= *Britannia Monogr*, 10.)

Fritz, G 1990 'Multiple pathways to farming in pre-contact eastern North America', *J World Prehist*, 4 (1990), 387–435.

Gallay, A 1990 'Historique des recherches entreprises sur la nécropole mégalithique du Petit-Chasseur à Sion (Valais, Suisse)', *in* Guilaine, J, & Gutherz, X (eds), *Autour de Jean Arnal*, 335–57. Montpellier: Univ des Sciences et Techniques du Languedoc.

Gardner, N 1925 *Olympia. Its history and remains*. Oxford: Clarendon Press.

Gendel, P 1984 *Mesolithic social territories in northwestern Europe*. Oxford: BAR. (= *BAR Int Ser*, 218).

Giot, PR 1971 'Circonscription de Bretagne', *Gallia Préhist*, 14 (1971), 339–61.

Giot, PR, L'Helgouac'h, J & Monnier, J-L 1979 *Préhistoire de la Bretagne*. Rennes: Ouest France.

Goody, J 1977 *The domestication of the savage mind*. Cambridge: Cambridge Univ Press.

Gould, R & Gould, E 1968 'Kunturu. An aboriginal sacred site on Lake Moore, Western Australia', *American Mus Novitates*, 2327 (1968), 1–17.

Graves, P 1989 'Social space in the English medieval parish church', *Economy and Society*, 18.3 (1989), 297–322.

Greber, N 1979 'A comparative study of site morphology and burial patterns at Edwin Harness Mound and Seip Mounds 1 and 2', in Brose, D & Greber, N (eds), *Hopewell Archaeology: the Chillicothe Conference*, 27–38. Kent: Kent State Univ Press.

Greenhalgh, M 1989 *The survival of Roman antiquities in the Middle Ages*. London: Duckworth.

Grinsell, L 1970 *The archaeology of Exmoor*. Newton Abbot: David & Charles.

Grosjean, R 1966 *La Corse avant l'histoire*. Paris: Editions Klincksieck.

Grosjean, R 1967 'Classification descriptive du mégalithique Corse: classification typologique et morphologique des menhirs et statues-menhirs de l'île', *Bull Soc Préhist Française*, 54 (1967), 707–42.

Grosjean, R 1972 'Les alignements de Pagliau (Sartène, Corse)', *Bull Soc Préhist Française*, 69 (1972), 607–17.

Haggarty, A 1988 'Machrie Moor', *Current Archaeol*, 109 (1988), 35–7.

Hameau, P 1989 *Les peintures postglaciares en Provence*. Paris: Editions de la Maison des Sciences de l'Homme.

Hamlin, A & Lynn, C 1988 *Pieces of the past*. Belfast: HMSO.

Harding, A 1981 'Excavations in the prehistoric ritual complex near Milfield, Northumberland', *Proc Prehist Soc*, 47 (1981), 87–135.

Hayden, B 1990 'Nimrods, piscators, pluckers and planters: the emergence of food production', *J Anthropol Archaeol*, 9 (1990), 31–69.

Headland, T & Reid, L 1989 Hunter gatherers and their neighbours from pre-history to the present', *Current Anthropol*, 30 (1989), 43–66.

Hedges, J & Buckley, D 1981 *The Springfield cursus and the cursus problem*. Chelmsford: Essex County Council. (= *Essex County Counc Occas Pap*, 1.)

Heggie, D 1981 *Megalithic science*. London: Thames & Hudson.

Hencken, H 1950 'Lagore Crannog: an Irish royal residence of the 7th to 10th centuries AD', *Proc Roy Ir Acad* C, 53 (1950), 1–248.

Hibbs, J 1984 'The Neolithic of Brittany and Normandy', *in* Scarre, C (ed), *Ancient France*, 271–323. Edinburgh: Edinburgh Univ Press.

Hill, P 1987 'Traprain Law: the Votadini and the Romans', *Scott Archaeol Rev*, 4.2 (1987), 85–91.

Hobley, B 1988 'Saxon London. Lundenwic and Lundenburgh: two cities rediscovered', in Hodges, R & Hobley, B (eds), *The rebirth of towns in the West, AD 700–1050*, 69–82. London: CBA. (= *CBA Res Rep*, 68.)

Hobsbawm, E 1983 'Inventing traditions', in Hobsbawm, E & Ranger, T (eds), *The invention of tradition*, 1–14. Cambridge: Cambridge Univ Press.

Hodder, I 1984 'Burials, houses, men and women in the European Neolithic', *in* Miller, D & Tilley, C (eds), *Ideology, power and prehistory*, 51–68. Cambridge: Cambridge Univ Press.

Hodder, I 1989 'This is not an article about material culture as text', *J Anthropol Archaeol*, 8 (1989), 250–69.

Hodder, I 1990 *The domestication of Europe*. Oxford: Blackwell.

Hodges, R 1982 *Dark Age economics*. London: Duckworth.

Hogg, A 1968 'Pen Llystyn: a Roman fort and other remains', *Archaeol J*, 125 (1968), 101–91.

Hope-Taylor, B 1977 *Yeavering. An Anglo-British centre of early Northumbria*. London: HMSO.

Hubert, F 1971 *Fossés Néolithiques à Spiennes*. (= *Archaeologia Belgica*, 136.)

Hunter, M 1974 'Germanic and Roman antiquity and the sense of the past in Anglo-Saxon England', *Anglo-Saxon England*, 3 (1974), 29–50.

Hvass, S 1991 'Jelling from Iron Age to Viking Age', *in* Wood, I & Lund, N (eds), *People and places in Northern Europe, 500–1600*, 149–60. Woodbridge: Boydell Press.

Ingold, T 1986 'Territoriality and tenure: the appropriation of space in hunting and gathering societies', *in* Ingold, T, *The appropriation of nature*, 130–64. Manchester: Manchester Univ Press.

Jallot, L & D'Anna, A 1990 'Stèles anthropomorphes et statues-menhirs: état de la question et approches méthodologiques nouvelles', *in* Guilaine, J & Gutherz, X (eds), *Autour de Jean Arnal*, 359–83. Montpellier: Univ des Sciences et Techniques de Languedoc.

Jehasse, J & Grosjean, R 1976 *Sites préhistoriques et protohistoriques de l'île de Corse*. Nice: Union Internationale des Sciences Préhistoriques et Protohistoriques.

Jennbert, K 1985 'Neolithicisation – a Scanian perspective', *J Danish Archaeol*, 4 (1985), 196–7.

Jensen, R 1989 'The Bronze Age in East Middle Sweden – heaps of fire-cracked stones and the settlement pattern', *in* Ambrosiani, B (ed), *Die Bronzezeit im Ostseegebiet*, 7–25. Stockholm: Almqvist & Wiksell.

Johnson, JS 1983 *Burgh Castle, excavations by Charles Green, 1958–61.* (= *E Anglian Archaeol*, 20.)

Johnston, S 1989 *Prehistoric Irish petroglyphs: their analysis and interpretation in anthropological context.* Ann Arbor: University Microfilms.

Jones, R 1977 'The Tasmanian paradox', *in* Wright, R (ed), *Stone tools as cultural markers*, 191–204. Canberra: Inst Aboriginal Stud.

Joussaume, R 1988 'Analyse structurale de la triple enceinte de fossés interrompus à Champ-Durand, Nieul-sur-l'Autize, Vendée', *in* Burgess, C, Topping, P, Mordant, C & Maddison, M (eds), *Enclosures and defences in the Neolithic of Western Europe*, 275–99. Oxford: BAR. (= *BAR Int Ser*, 403).

Joussaume, R & Pautreau, J-P 1990 *Le Préhistoire du Poitou.* Tours: Editions Ouest-France.

Kalb, P 1989 'Überlagen zu Neolithisierung und Megalithik in Western der Iberishen Halbisnsel', *Madrider Mitteilungen*, 30 (1989), 31–54.

Keeley, L 1992 'The introduction of agriculture to the western North European plain', *in* Gebauer, AB & Price, TD (eds), *Transitions to agriculture in prehistory*, 81–95. Madison: Prehistory Press. (= *Monogr in World Archaeol* 4.)

Keeley, L & Cahen, D 1989 'Early Neolithic forts and villages in north-east Belgium: a preliminary report', *J Field Archaeol*, 16 (1989), 157–76.

Kemp, R 1987 'Anglian York – the missing link', *Current Archaeol*, 104 (1987), 259–63.

Kemp, W 1991 'Visual narratives, memory and the medieval *esprit du système*', *in* Küchler, S & Melion, W (eds), *Images of memory: on remembering and representation*, 87–108. Washington: Smithsonian Institution Press.

Kinnes, I 1992 *Non-megalithic long barrows and allied structures in the British Isles.* London: Brit Mus. (= *Brit Mus Occas Pap*, 52.)

Kinnes, I & Hibbs, J 1989 'Le Gardien du Tombeau: further reflections on the initial Neolithic', *Oxford J Archaeol*, 8 (1989), 159–66.

Küchler, S 1987 'Malangan – art and memory in a Melanesian society', *Man*, 22 (1987), 238–55.

Kuper, R & Piepers, W 1966 ' Ein Siedlung der Rössener Kultur in Inden und Lamersdorf', *Bonner Jahrbuch*, 174 (1966), 424–508.

Kuper, R, Löhr, H, Lüning, J, Stehli, P & Zimmerman, A 1977 *Die Bandkeramische Siedlungplatz Langweiler 9.* Bonn: Habelt.

Lambrick, G 1990 'Ritual and burial in the Thames Valley', *Current Archaeol*, 121 (1990), 6–13.

Larsson, L 1990a 'The Mesolithic of Southern Scandinavia', *J World Prehist*, 4 (1990), 257–309.

Larsson, L 1990b 'Symbols in action – dogs in fraction', in Veermeersch, P & Van Peer, P (eds), *Contributions to the Mesolithic in Europe*, 153–60. Leuven: Leuven Univ Press.

Layton, R 1986 'Political and territorial structures among hunter gatherers', *Man*, 21 (1986), 18–33.

Leroi-Gourhan, A 1965 *Préhistoire de l'art occidental.* Paris: Mazenod.

Le Roux, C-T 1984 'A propos de fouilles de Gavrinis (Morbihan): nouvelles données sur l'art mégalithique Armoricain', *Bull Soc Préhist Française*, 81 (1984), 240–5.

Le Roux, C-T, Lecerf, Y & Gautier, M 1989 'Les mégalithes de Saint-Just (Ile et Vilaine) et la fouille des alignements du Moulin de Cojou', *Rev Archéol de l'Ouest*, 6 (1989), 5–29.

Le Rouzic, Z 1927 Depôts rituels de haches en pierre poli découverts dans le region de Carnac', *Bull Soc Préhist Française*, 24 (1927), 156–60.

Le Rouzic, Z 1930 *Les Cromlechs de Er-Lannic.* Vannes.

L'Helgouac'h, J 1965 *Les sépultures mégalithiques en Armorique.* Rennes: Travaux du Laboratoire d'Anthropologie Préhistorique.

L'Helgouac'h, J 1976 'Le tumulus de Dissignac à Saint-Nazaire (Loire-Atlantique) et les problèmes du contact entre le phenoméne mégalithique et les sociétés à l'industrie microlithique', *in* De Laet, S (ed), *Acculturation and continuity in Atlantic Europe*, 142–9. Bruges: De Tempel.

L'Helgouac'h, J 1983 'Les idoles qu'on abat', *Bull Soc Polymathique du Morbihan*, (1983), 57–68.

L'Helgouac'h, J 1988 'Le site Néolithique final à fossés interrompus des prises à Machcoul, Loire Atlantique', *in* Burgess, C, Topping, P, Mordant, C & Maddison, M (eds), *Enclosures and defences in the Neolithic of Western Europe*, 265–73. Oxford: BAR. (= *BAR Int Ser*, 403.)

Lindqvist, S 1936 *Uppsala Högar och Ottarshögen.* Stockholm: Wahlström & Widstrand.

Lombardo, J-C, Martinez, R & Verret, D 1984 'Le site Chasséen de Culfroid à Boury-en-Vexin dans son contexte historique et les apports de la stratigraphie de son fossé', *Rev Archéol de Picardie*, 1.2 (1984), 269–92.

Lourandos, H 1988 'Palaeopolitics: resource intensification in Aboriginal Australia and Papua New Guinea', *in* Ingold, T, Riches, D & Woodburn, J (eds), *Hunters and gatherers: history, evolution and social change*, 148–60. Oxford: Berg.

Lüning, J 1967 'Die Michelsberg Kultur. Ihre Funde in zeitlicher und räumlicher Gliederung', *Bericht der Römisch-Germanischen Kommission*, 48 (1967), 1–350.

Lüning, J 1982 'Research into the Bandkeramik settlement in the Aldenhoven Platte in the Rhineland', *Analecta Praehistorica Leidensia*, 15 (1982), 1–29.

Lüning, J 1988 'Zur Verbreitung und Datierung bandkeramischer Erdwerk', *Archäologisches Korrespondenzblatt*, 18 (1988), 155–8.

Lynch, F 1991 *Prehistoric Anglesey*, 2 edn. Llangefni: Anglesey Antiq Soc.

Lynn, C 1986 'Navan Fort: a draft summary of DM Waterman's excavation', *Emainia*, 1 (1986), 11–19.

MacKie, E 1977 *Science and society in prehistoric Britain.* London: Elek.

MacKie, E & Davis, A 1989 'New light on Neolithic rock carvings: the petroglyphs at Greenland (Auchentorlie), Dunbartonshire', *Glasgow Archaeol J*, 15 (1988–9), 125–55.

Madsen, T 1982 'Settlement systems of early agricultural societies in East Jutland, Denmark: a regional study of change', *J Anthropol Archaeol*, 1 (1982), 197–236.

Madsen, T 1988 'Causewayed enclosures in South Scandinavia', *in* Burgess, C, Topping, P, Mordant C & Maddison, M (eds), *Enclosures and defences in the Neolithic of Western Europe*, 301–36. Oxford: BAR. (= *BAR Int Ser*, 403).

Mallory, J & Hartwell, B 1984 'Donegore', *Current Archaeol*, 92 (1984), 271–5.

Malmer, M 1981 *A chorological study of North European rock art*. Stockholm: Almqvist & Wiksell.

Malone, C 1985 'Pots, prestige and ritual in Neolithic southern Italy', *in* Malone, C & Stoddard, S (eds), *Papers in Italian archaeology, 4 pt 2: Prehistory*, 118–51. Oxford: BAR. (= *BAR Int Ser*, 244.)

Manby, T 1976 'Excavation of the Kilham long barrow, East Riding of Yorkshire', *Proc Prehist Soc*, 42 (1976), 111–59.

Manby, T 1986 *The Thwing project: excavation and field archaeology in East Yorkshire*. York: Yorkshire Archaeol Soc.

Manby, T 1988 'The Neolithic period in eastern Yorkshire', *in* Manby, T (ed), *Archaeology in Eastern Yorkshire*, 35–88. Sheffield: Sheffield Univ Dept Archaeol Préhist.

Marolle, C 1989 'Le village Michelsberg des Hautes Chanvières à Mairy (Ardennes)', *Gallia Préhist*, 31 (1989), 93–117.

Meillassoux, C 1972 'From reproduction to production', *Economy and Society*, 1 (1972), 93–105.

Melion, W & Küchler, S 1991 'Introduction: memory, cognition and image production', *in* Küchler, S & Melion, W (eds) *Images of memory: on remembering and representation*, 1–46. Washington: Smithsonian Institution Press.

Mellars, P 1987 *Excavations on Oronsay. Prehistoric human ecology on a small island*. Edinburgh: Edinburgh Univ Press.

Mellars, P 1991 'Technological changes across the Middle – Upper Palaeolithic transition: economic, social and cognitive perspectives', *in* Mellars, P & Stringer, C (eds), *The human revolution*, 338–65. Edinburgh: Edinburgh Univ Press.

Mercer, R 1981 'Excavations at Carn Brea, Illogan, Cornwall – a Neolithic fortified complex of the third millennium bc', *Cornish Archaeol*, 20 (1981), 1–204.

Mercer, R 1988 'Hambledon Hill, Dorset, England', *in* Burgess, C, Topping, P, Mordant C & Maddison, M (eds), *Enclosures and defences in the Neolithic of Western Europe*, 89–106. Oxford: BAR. (= *BAR Int Ser*, 403).

Mezzena, F 1981 'Le Valle d'Aosta nella preistoria e nella protostoria', *in* *Archaeologia in Valle d'Aosta*, 15–60. Aosta: Regione Valle d'Aosta Assessorat del Turisma Urbanistica e Beni Culturali.

Miket, R 1981 'Pit alignments in the Milfield Basin and the excavation of Ewart 1', *Proc Prehist Soc*, 47 (1981), 137–46.

Miket, R 1985 'Ritual enclosures on Whitton Hill, Northumberland', *Proc Prehist Soc*, 51 (1985), 137–48.

Miles, H 1975 'Barrows on the St Austell granite', *Cornish Archaeol*, 14 (1975), 5–81.

Miln, J 1881 *Fouilles faites à Carnac (Bretagne)*. Rennes: Typographie Oberthur.

Modderman, P 1958 'Die bandkeramische Siedlung von Sittard', *Palaeohistoria*, 6 (1958), 33–120.

Mordant, D & Mordant, C 1977 'Habitat néolithique de fond de vallée alluviale à Noyen-sur-Seine (Seine-et-Marne): Etude archéologique', *Gallia Préhist*, 20 (1977), 229–69.

Moreland, J & Van de Noort, R 1992 'Integration and social reproduction in the Carolingian empire', *World Archaeol*, 23 (1992), 320–34.

Morgan, C 1990 *Athletes and oracles: the transformation of Olympia and Delphi in the 8th Century BC*. Cambridge: Cambridge Univ Press.

Morphy, H 1991 *Ancestral Connections*. Chicago: Chicago Univ Press.

Muller, J 1987 'Salt, chert and shell: Mississippian exchange and economy', *in* Brumfiel, E & Earle, T (eds), *Specialisation and exchange in complex societies*, 10–21. Cambridge: Cambridge Univ Press.

O'Hare, G 1990 'A preliminary study of polished stone artefacts in prehistoric southern Italy', *Proc Prehist Soc*, 56 (1990), 123–52.

O'Kelly, M 1982 *Newgrange. Archaeology, art and legend*. London: Thames & Hudson.

O'Kelly, M, Cleary, R & Lehane, D 1983 *Newgrange, Co Meath, Ireland: the Late Neolithic / Beaker period settlement*. Oxford: BAR. (= *BAR Int Ser*, 190.)

O'Kelly, M & O'Kelly, C 1983 'The tumulus at Dowth, Co Meath', *Proc Roy Ir Acad C*, 78 (1983), 136–90.

O'Riordain, S 1957 *Tara: the monuments on the hill*. Dundalk: Dundalgan Press.

O'Sullivan, M 1986 'Approaches to passage tomb art', *J Roy Soc Antiq Ir*, 116 (1986), 68–83.

Patrik, J 1981 'A reassessment of the solstitial observations at Kintraw and Ballochroy', *in* Ruggles, C & Whittle, A (eds), *Astronomy and society during the period 4000 – 1500 BC*, 211–19. Oxford: BAR. (= *BAR Brit Ser*, 88.)

Patton, M 1987 *Jersey in prehistory*. Jersey: La Haule Books.

Patton, M 1990 'Dynamics of culture change in Neolithic communities: an Armorican case study', *Bull Univ London Inst Archaeol*, 27 (1990), 61–85.

Patton, M 1991 'An Early Neolithic axe factory at Le Pinacle, Jersey, Channel Islands', *Proc Prehist Soc*, 57.2 (1991), 51–9.

Peña Santos, A & Vàzquez Varela, JM 1979 *Los Petroglifos Gallegos*. La Coruña: Edicios do Castro.

Perzigian, A, Tench, P & Brawn, D 1984 'Prehistoric health in the Ohio river valley', *in* Cohen, M & Armelagos, G (eds), *Palaeopathology at the origins of agriculture*, 347–66. New York: Academic Press.

Pitts, M 1982 'On the road to Stonehenge: report on the investigations beside the A344 in 1968, 1979 and 1980', *Proc Prehist Soc*, 48 (1982), 75–132.

Proudfoot, VB 1955 *The Downpatrick gold find*. Belfast: HMSO.

Proudfoot, VB 1957 'A second gold find from Downpatrick', *Ulster J Archaeol*, 20 (1957), 70–2.

Pryor, F in press '"Abandonment" and the role of ritual sites in the landscape', *Scott Archaeol Rev*.

Pryor, F & French, C 1985 *Archaeology and environment in the Lower Welland Valley*. (= *E Anglian Archaeol*, 27.)

RCAHMS 1988 Royal Commission on the Ancient and Historical Monuments of Scotland, *Argyll, an inventory of the monuments, vol 6: mid Argyll and Cowal*. Edinburgh: HMSO.

RCAHMS 1990 Royal Commission on the Ancient and Historical Monuments of Scotland, *North-east Perth: an archaeological landscape*. Edinburgh: HMSO.

RCHME 1975 Royal Commission on Historical Monuments (England), *County of Dorset*, vol 5: *East Dorset*. London: HMSO.

RCHME 1979 Royal Commission on Historical Monuments (England), *Stonehenge and its environs*. Edinburgh: Edinburgh Univ Press.

Raetzel-Fabian, D 1991 'Zwischen Fluchtburg und Kultstätte', *Archäologie in Deutschland*, 4 (Oct–Dec 1991), 22–5.

Rahtz, P & Watts, L 1979 'The end of Roman temples in the west of Britain', *in* Casey, J (ed), *The end of Roman Britain*, 183–201. Oxford: BAR. (= *BAR Brit Ser*, 71.)

Rapinot, J-C 1986 'Informations archéologiques: Poitou – Charente', *Gallia Préhist*, 29 (1986), 443–71.

Raschke, W 1988 'Images of victory: some new considerations of athletic monuments', *in* Raschke, W (ed), *The archaeology of the Olympics*, 38–54. Madison: Univ Wisconsin Press.

Renfrew, C 1973 *Before civilization*. London: Cape.

Renfrew, C 1985 'Epilogue', *in* Renfrew, C (ed), *The prehistory of Orkney*, 243–61. Edinburgh: Edinburgh Univ Press.

Richards, C 1991 'Skara Brae: revisiting a Neolithic village', *in* Hanson, W & Slater, E (eds), *Scottish archaeology: new perceptions*, 24–43. Aberdeen: Aberdeen Univ Press.

Richards, J 1990 *The Stonehenge Environs Project*. London: Historic Buildings & Monuments Commission. (= *HBMC Archaeol Rep*, 16.)

Riley, D 1988 'Air survey of Neolithic sites on the Yorkshire Wolds', *in* Manby, T (ed), *Archaeology in Eastern Yorkshire*, 89–93. Sheffield: Univ Sheffield Dept Archaeol Prehist.

Rose, J, Burnett, B, Blaeuer, M & Nassaney, M 1984 'Palaeopathology and the origins of maize cultivation in the lower Mississippi and Caddoan areas', *in* Cohen, M & Armelagos, G (eds), *Palaeopathology at the origins of agriculture*, 393–424. New York: Academic Press.

Ruggles, C 1984 *Megalithic astronomy. A new archaeological and statistical study of 300 western Scottish sites*. Oxford: BAR. (= *BAR Brit Ser*, 123.)

Ruggles, C & Burl, A 1985 'A new study of the Aberdeenshire recumbent stone circles, 2: interpretation', *Archaeoastronomy*, 8 (1985), 25–60.

Saville, A 1990 *Hazleton North. The excavation of a long cairn of the Cotswold-Severn group*. London: Historic Buildings and Monuments Commission. (= *HBMC Archaeol Rep*, 13.)

Scarre, C 1992 'The Early Neolithic of western France and megalithic origins in Atlantic Europe', *Oxford J Archaeol*, 11 (1992), 121–54.

Scollar, I 1959 'A Neolithic enclosure at Spiennes, Belgium', *Antiquity*, 29 (1959), 159–61.

Scott, J 1989 'The stone circle at Temple Wood, Kilmartin, Argyll', *Glasgow Archaeol J*, 15 (1988–9), 53–124.

Scull, C & Harding, A 1990 'Two early medieval cemeteries at Milfield, Northumberland', *Durham Archaeol J*, 6 (1990), 1–29.

Sharples, N 1984 'Excavations at Pierowall Quarry, Westray, Orkney', *Proc Soc Antiq Scot*, 114 (1984), 75–125, fiche 1:D3–2:G5.

Sharples, N 1991 *Maiden Castle. Excavations and field survey 1985–6*. London: Historic Buildings & Monuments Commission. (= *HBMC Archaeol Rep*, 19.)

Shee, E 1972 'Three decorated stones from Loughcrew, Co Meath', *J Roy Soc Antiq Ir*, 102 (1972), 224–33.

Shee Twohig, E 1981 *The megalithic art of Western Europe*. Oxford: Clarendon Press.

Shennan, S 1983 'Monuments: an example of archaeologists' use of the massively material', *Roy Anthropol Inst Newsletter*, 59 (1983), 9–11.

Shennan, S, Healy, F & Smith, I 1985 'The excavation of a ring ditch in Tye Field, Lawford, Essex', *Archaeol J*, 142 (1985), 150–215.

Sheridan, A 1986 'Porcellanite artefacts: a new survey', *Ulster J Archaeol*, 49 (1986), 19–32.

Sherratt, A 1990 'The genesis of megaliths: ethnicity and social complexity in Neolithic northwest Europe', *World Archaeol*, 22 (1990), 147–67.

Sherratt, A 1991 'Sacred and profane substances: the ritual use of narcotics in Later Neolithic Europe', *in* Garwood, P, Jennings, D, Skeates, R & Toms, J (eds), *Sacred and profane*, 50–64. Oxford: Oxford Univ Committee for Archaeol.

Simpson, D 1989 'Neolithic Navan?', *Emainia*, 6 (1989), 31–3.

Sisam, K 1990 'Anglo-Saxon royal genealogies', *in* Stanley, E (ed), *British Academy papers on Anglo-Saxon England*, 145–204. Oxford: Oxford Univ Press.

Skeates, R 1991 'Caves, cult and children in Neolithic Abruzzo, central Italy', *in* Garwood, P, Jennings, D, Skeates, R & Toms, J (eds), *Sacred and profane*, 122–34. Oxford: Oxford Univ Committee for Archaeol.

Smith, I 1965 *Windmill Hill and Avebury*. Oxford: Clarendon Press.

Snodgrass, A 1986 'Interaction by design: the Greek city state', *in* Renfrew, C & Cherry, J (eds), *Peer polity interaction and sociopolitical complexity*, 47–58. Cambridge: Cambridge Univ Press.

Spratt, D 1982 *Prehistoric and Roman archaeology of North-east Yorkshire*. Oxford: BAR. (= *BAR Brit Ser*, 104.)

Steane, K 1992 'St Paul in the Bail', *Current Archaeol*, 129 (1992), 376–9.

Steer, K & Bannerman, J 1977 *Late Medieval monumental sculpture in the West Highlands*. Edinburgh: HMSO.

Stone, JFS 1935 'Some discoveries at Ratfyn, Amesbury and their bearing on the date of Woodhenge', *Wiltshire Archaeol Mag*, 47 (1935), 55–67.

Strauss, L 1991 'The "Mesolithic – Neolithic transition" in Portugal: a view from Vidigal', *Antiquity*, 65 (1991), 899–903.

Strickertsson, K, Sanderson, D, Placido, F & Tate, J 1988 'The thermoluminescence dating of Scottish vitrified forts: new results and a review', *in* Slater, E & Tate, J (eds), *Science and archaeology, Glasgow 1987*, 625–33. Oxford: BAR. (= *BAR Brit Ser*, 196.)

Stuart, J 1864 *Memoir of Alexander Henry Rhind of Sibster*. Edinburgh: Soc Antiq Scot.

Sweetman, D 1985 'A Late Neolithic / Early Bronze Age pit circle at Newgrange, Co Meath', *Proc Royal Ir Acad C*, 85 (1985), 195–221.

Thevenot, J-P 1985 'Informations archéologiques: circonscription de Bourgogne', *Gallia Préhist*, 28 (1985), 171–210.

Thevenot, J-P, Gaillard de Sémainville, H, Mazingue, B & Depierre, G 1988 'Circonscription de Bourgogne', *Gallia Informations*, (1987–8 pt 2), 1–74.

Thom, A & Thom, AS 1978 *Megalithic remains in Britain and Brittany*. Oxford: Clarendon Press.

Thom, A, Thom, AS & Burl, A 1990 *Stone rows and standing stones*. Oxford: BAR. (= *BAR Int Ser*, 560.)

Thomas, C 1964 'The Society's 1962 excavations: the henge at Castilly, Lanivet', *Cornish Archaeol*, 3 (1964), 3–14.

Thomas, J 1991 *Rethinking the Neolithic*. Cambridge: Cambridge Univ Press.

Thomas, J 1992 'Monuments, movement and the context of megalithic art', *in* Sharples, N & Sheridan, A (eds), *Vessels for the ancestors*, 143–55. Edinburgh: Edinburgh Univ Press.

Thomas, J & Whittle, A 1986 'Anatomy of a tomb – West Kennet revisited', *Oxford J Archaeol*, 5 (1986), 129–56.

Thomas, K 1982 'Neolithic enclosures and woodland habitats on the South Downs', *in* Bell, M & Limbrey, S (eds), *Archaeological aspects of woodland ecology*, 147–70. Oxford: BAR. (= *BAR Suppl Ser*, 146.)

Thrane, H 1989 'Danish ploughmarks from the Neolithic and Bronze Age', *J Danish Archaeol*, 8 (1989), 111–25.

Tilley, C 1989 'Hunter gatherers, farmers and the social structuring of material culture', *in* Larsson, T & Lundmark, H (eds), *Approaches to Swedish prehistory*, 239–86. Oxford: BAR. (= *BAR Int Ser*, 500.)

Tinniswood, A & Harding, A 1991 'Anglo-Saxon occupation and industrial features in the henge monument at Yeavering, Northumberland', *Durham Archaeol J*, 7 (1991), 93–108.

Trigger, B 1990 'Monumental architecture: a thermodynamic explanation of symbolic behaviour', *World Archaeol*, 22 (1990), 119–32.

Trnka, G 1991 *Studien zu mittelneolithischen Kreisgrabenanlagen*. Vienna: Osterreichischen Akademie der Wissenschaften.

Ucko, P, Hunter, M, Clark, A & David, A 1991 *Avebury reconsidered*. London: Unwin Hyman.

Van Berg, P-L 1991 'Géometrie de quelque enceintes fossoyés du Runabé récent rhéno-mosan', *Actes du Quinzième Colloque Interrégionale sur le Néolithique*, 25–32. Voirpreux: Association Régional pour la Protection et l'Etude du Patrimonie Préhistorique.

Vaquer, J 1990 *Le Néolithique en Languedoc Occidental*. Paris: Editions de Centre National de la Recherche Scientifique.

Veermeersch, P & Walter, R 1980 *Thieusies, Ferme de l'Hosté, site Michelsberg*. (= *Archéol Belgica*, 230.)

Waddell, J 1988 'Rathcroghan in Connacht', *Emainia*, 5 (1988), 5–18.

Wailes, B 1982 'The Irish "royal" sites in history and archaeology', *Cambridge Medieval Celtic Stud*, 3 (1982), 1–29.

Wailes, B 1990 'Dún Ailinne: a summary excavation report', *Emainia*, 7 (1990), 10–21.

Wainwright, G 1979 *Mount Pleasant, Dorset. Excavations 1970 – 1971.* London: Society of Antiquaries. (= *Soc Antiq London Res Rep*, 37.)

Wainwright, G & Longworth, I 1971 *Durrington Walls. Excavations 1966 and 1968.* London: Society of Antiquaries. (= *Soc Antiq London Res Rep*, 29.)

Ward-Perkins, B 1984 *From classical antiquity to the Middle Ages. Urban public building in Northern and Central Italy.* Oxford: Oxford Univ Press.

Warner, R 1976 'Some observations on the context and importation of exotic material in Ireland, from the first century BC to the second century AD', *Proc Roy Ir Acad C*, 76 (1976), 267–92.

Warner, R 1988 'The archaeology of Early Historic Irish kingship', *in* Driscoll, S & Nieke, M (eds), *Power and politics in Early Medieval Britain and Ireland*, 47–68. Edinburgh: Edinburgh Univ Press.

Whitehouse, R 1990 'Caves and cult in Neolithic southern Italy', *in* Herring, E, Whitehouse, R & Wilkins, J (eds), *Accordia Res Pap*, 1, 19–37. London: Accordia Research Centre.

Whittle, A 1977 'Earlier Neolithic enclosures in north-west Europe', *Proc Prehist Soc*, 43 (1977), 329–48.

Whittle, A 1985 *Neolithic Europe: a survey.* Cambridge: Cambridge Univ Press.

Whittle, A 1988 *Problems in Neolithic archaeology.* Cambridge: Cambridge Univ Press.

Whittle, A 1991 'A Late Neolithic complex at West Kennet, Wiltshire, England', *Antiquity*, 65 (1991), 256–62.

Williams, R 1989 *People of the Black Mountains. 1: The beginning.* London: Chatto & Windus.

Wilmott, T 1989 'Birdoswald – Dark Age halls in a Roman fort?', *Current Archaeol*, 116 (1989), 288–91.

Wilson, P 1988 *The domestication of the human species.* New Haven: Yale Univ Press.

Woodburn, J 1982 'Egalitarian societies', *Man*, 17 (1982), 431–45.

Woodburn, J 1988 'African hunter gatherer social organisation: is it best understood as a product of encapsulation?', *in* Ingold, T, Riches, D & Woodburn, J (eds), *Hunters and gatherers – history, evolution and social change*, 31–64. Oxford: Berg.

Woodward, P, Davis, S & Graham, A 1984 'Excavations at Greyhound Yard car-park, Dorchester, 1984', *Proc Dorset Natur Hist Achaeol Soc*, 106 (1984), 99–106.

Woodward, P & Smith, R 1987 'Survey and excavation along the route of the southern Dorchester by-pass, 1986–7: an interim note. *Proc Dorset Natur Hist Archaeol Soc*, 109 (1987), 79–89.

Young, R 1989 'Mixed lithic scatters and the Mesolithic – Neolithic transition in the northeast of England: a speculation', *in* Brooks, I & Phillips, P (eds), *Breaking the stony silence*, 161–85. Oxford: BAR. (= *BAR Brit Ser*, 213.)

Zammit, T 1930 'The prehistoric remains of the Maltese islands', *Antiquity*, 4 (1930), 55–79.

Zvelebil, M & Rowley-Conwy, P 1986 'Foragers and farmers in Atlantic Europe', in Zvelebil, M (ed), *Hunters in transition*, 67–93. Cambridge: Cambridge Univ Press.

INDEX